BODY WORSHIP

Postures of Praise

Timothy Sohn

Dedicated to my father,
who is now in Heaven,
singing his heart out in praise.

My dream was to work on this book with you,
but the Lord brought you home first;
I hope it makes you proud.

Someday soon I will see you again,
and we will kneel together in worship
before the throne of God.

CONTENTS

BODY WORSHIP

Therefore, I urge you,
brothers and sisters,
in view of God's mercy,
to offer your bodies as a living sacrifice,
holy and pleasing to God –
This is your true and proper worship.
(Romans 12:1, NIV)

God is worthy of all worship. We were created to worship God. Let us worship Him with all that we are, and as we do so, may our knowledge and awe of who He is continue to expand, and naturally our understanding of what it means to worship God will continually grow.

The act of worship is to bestow worth upon someone or something - to declare the object of worship as being worthy. Worship today in the modern church is often associated with congregational singing, but the true nature of the act is so much bigger than just music. Some of the most beautiful worship can happen in silence. There is a plethora of ways to convey worth that do not require words or sounds. And in the same way that human-to-human communication can happen without speaking, the body language we use while giving praise can also impart meaning and truth well beyond our words and songs.

Body Language

Humans have the innate ability to communicate very effectively through body language - we know what it means when arms are crossed or when fists are clenched, and from a very early age we understand the importance of eye contact. We can tell how a person is feeling from the way that they are standing, their facial expression, or how their hands are positioned. If a picture is worth a thousand words, how many words can a gesture convey?

Consider the humble thumbs-up sign, typically used to convey approval, a well-known gesture in many cultures around the world. Its popularity can be traced back through its use by fighter pilots during World War II, all the way back to the gladiatorial contests of Ancient Rome, or even earlier in history. Though instantly familiar, its exact origins have been lost from our collective memory. Now, we can only guess as to how this particular signal, of a closed fist with raised thumb, first became associated with the positive message that we use it for today. The same can be said for the OK sign, the peace sign, or any number of other hand signals, but regardless of their mysterious inceptions, they all broadcast meaningful messages nonverbally, yet very effectively.

Even the rise in popularity of memes on social media points to our ability to silently communicate with each other - instead of expressing what you are feeling through words, now you can simply post something online that instantly shares your emotions. Feeling down? Post a Sad Keanu meme. Feeling optimistic? Post a Success Kid meme. Post one of a countless number of memes online, and a stranger halfway across the world, without shared language or culture, can instantly know exactly how you feel - all without any exchange of words.

Similarly, our body postures can broadcast a wide range of meanings to those around us. For example, a bowed head is a posture that displays defeat - picture a husband who has just lost his job, unsure of how to put into words his sadness and shame to his family. Or picture a baseball team who just lost on the very last play of the game - so close to victory, but now going back home having squandered an opportunity. Without saying anything, you know instantly how they feel inside, just by the way their bodies are positioned.

This ability is not limited only to human-to-human interaction; we can also use this skill to communicate with God and expand our expression of praise. If singing in praise is worshipping the Lord through spoken language, then praising through the posture of our bodies is worshipping God through unspoken language. And when we find ourselves in times of worship where it seems like our words are falling short of what we're trying to say, then we can use these postures of praise to express what we are feeling inside that we could not say through songs and lyrics alone.

Posture in the Bible

Consider the story in the Book of Luke, where Jesus describes the posture of a Pharisee, proudly standing in public prayer, gladly showing off his pretense of piety to all those around. In the story, he is juxtaposed with a sinful tax collector who approaches the temple remorsefully, ashamed to even show his face. "'Two men went up to the temple to pray, one a Pharisee and the other a tax collector. The Pharisee stood by himself and prayed: 'God, I thank you that I am not like other people - robbers, evildoers, adulterers - or even like this tax collector. I fast twice a week and give a tenth of all I get.' But the tax collector stood at a distance. He would not even look up to heaven, but beat his breast and said, 'God, have mercy on me, a sinner'" (Luke 18:10-13, NIV). Just by looking at their body positions, it is easy to identify which man was coming before the Lord with the right heart attitude.

We see in this parable that God is looking past outward acts of service and devotion - more than these things, He desires His people to be repentant inside and to acknowledge that we are in desperate need of His grace. Outwardly, the Pharisee would have been considered the more righteous of the two, but somehow it was the lowly sinner who had the heart of worship that God wanted, which was displayed through his penitent posture. Jesus explained to His followers, "'I tell you that this man, rather than the other, went home justified before God. For all those who exalt themselves will be humbled, and those who humble themselves will be exalted'" (Luke 18:14, NIV). The tax collector's bowed head revealed the humility and guilt of his heart, and his faith was rewarded with forgiveness.

Even the language used in the Bible reflects the power of posture in communication. One of the main words used in the New Testament that is translated into English as the word for worship is Proskuneo, a Greek word that means to bow down. Similarly, Shachah is a Hebrew word that is often used as the word for worship in the Old Testament, and it also means to bow down.

Bowing is to bend and lower the body as a reflection of the heart, to declare that the One being bowed before is worthy of honor and glory, and higher than ourselves. We bow down before our Lord because He is our Creator, Savior, and King; He is worthy of worship simply for being the great I AM (Exodus 3:14). When we bow in worship, we echo the words of John the Baptist, who said of Jesus Christ, "He must become greater; I must become less" (John 3:30, NIV).

So many of the words used in Biblical teaching have physical and tangible meanings, while at the same time conveying deep spiritual significance as well. They paint a picture of what the word means, and Proskuneo is such a great example of this. Worship is not just something that happens in the heart or mind alone, or just through lifting our voices up in song. There is also this physical and tangible way that the Lord desires His people to worship Him - one method pleasing to God is to bow down before Him, though bowing is just one example of a posture of praise.

God loves to give His people object lessons to teach them about His nature, and how to live according to His will. Sabbath, fasting, circumcision, baptism, sacrifices - all physical and tangible acts that paint profound spiritual pictures of what it means to have faith, to trust in Him alone, and to be devoted and set apart as His people. Proskuneo is another of these object lessons: God is teaching us that the call to worship is more than just a call to music, it is a call to use our whole being - soul and body - to declare the Lord as worthy.

How to Worship

There is no definitive manual on how to worship, nor would one ever be needed. Humans do not need to learn how to worship - we exist to worship, we were born with the ability to worship, and it is innately within us as created beings to worship our

Creator. Sadly though, that holy desire to worship has been twisted and turned by sin into the worship of other, lesser gods - this was true during Biblical times, and it remains true to this very day.

Everybody worships - it is not a particularly Christian or even religious activity. Every human worships something or someone. We are constantly rendering worthiness, both consciously and sub-consciously, whether it is to a person, an ideological belief, a political system, a religion, wealth, power, or anything else that people chase after. This human need to worship is like being a planet in the solar system, forever locked in rotation around the sun. We exist under a constant gravitational pull, and are compelled by our nature to spend our lives orbiting around something bigger than ourselves.

We do not need to learn how to worship, rather it is <u>Who</u> to worship that we must be con-tinuously reminded of, and recalibrate towards. We can spend our days revolving around lesser gods that are not worthy, or we can shift our trajectory to place God at the center of our lives. He alone is truly worthy of worship, and we are called to give all that we have in praise to Him, as it is written in the Bible, "You shall worship the Lord your God and him only shall you serve" (Matthew 4:10, ESV).

If there were something like a manual on true worship, it would have to be the Bible, the liv-ing Word of God. The Lord has filled those pages with descriptions of the kind of worship that He de-sires, and with examples of the heart attitude that we should have when approaching Him. God has plainly revealed from the very beginning what it is that He wants from His people. We can see this from the Shema Yisrael prayer: "Hear, O Israel: The Lord our God, the Lord is one. Love the Lord your God with all your heart and with all your soul and with all your strength" (Deuteronomy 6:4-5, NIV). Our Creator God formed us to worship and love Him with everything that we are, and we find satisfaction and purpose in life by using all that we have, spiritual and physical, to give Him praise.

Part of our worship is to offer the Lord songs of praise, as the Bible encourages us, "Sing and make music from your heart to the Lord, always giving thanks to God the Father for everything, in the name of our Lord Jesus Christ" (Ephesians 5:19-20, NIV). However, it is not merely singing that God desires from us - He wants everything we have. Our hearts, minds, souls, and bodies all belong to Him alone.

God is looking into the deepest parts of our being - and our bodies reveal much about what is inside. That is why our postures during praise are so important; our body worship is an integral part of the way that we glorify the Lord. The Apostle Paul reinforces this truth to us: "Therefore, I urge you, brothers and sisters, in view of God's mercy, to offer your bodies as a living sacrifice, holy and pleasing to God - This is your true and proper worship" (Romans 12:1, NIV). The postures of our bodies reflect the orientation of our hearts, and so they are an essential part of the offering of praise that we bring before the Lord.

The Bible also describes for us the kind of worship that the Lord does not desire. In the Book of Amos, God seems to despise the musical worship that He had been receiving from the people of Israel, because it was devoid of what He truly wanted. The Lord declared, "Away with the noise of your songs! I will not listen to the music of your harps. But let justice roll on like a river, righteousness like a never-failing stream!" (Amos 5:23-24, NIV).

It was the Lord Himself who had commanded Israel to worship Him with songs, but when they did so with unrepentant hearts, He rejected their praise and sacrifices. The music and singing alone, no matter how beautiful, were not enough for Him. God wanted the words they were professing to match their heart-attitudes, and that righteous desire remains to this day. In the same way, we can be sure that God would easily see past any posture of praise put on simply for show, without a true heart of worship behind it.

The praise that the Lord desires does not require one to be morally perfect and without sin. If we are penitent before Him, then our adoration will not be rejected, as the Psalmist wrote, "The sacrifices of God are a broken spirit; a broken and contrite heart, O God, you will not despise" (Psalms 51:17, ESV). The Lord desires worship, but not from a people who will praise Him one moment only to turn away from His commands later - God wants us to commit sincerely and full-heartedly when we approach His throne.

Body Worship

There are times when our bodies will move without thought in worship, purely out of instinct - but there are also times when we feel called to move in a more intentional way. In many ways it is reminiscent of the codes of conduct and etiquette required when being presented before human kings and queens. Monarchial cultures and traditions have outlined certain requirements for commoners to behave by, such as greeting with a bow or curtsy, addressing the royals by specific titles, or only speaking when spoken to. These kinds of rules are in place as a reminder that the sovereign is of a higher status than the rest of the population. If this is the standard for how to act when approaching human kings, then it would follow that we should show even greater deference when approaching the King of Kings.

We see throughout the Old Testament that there were expectations placed upon those who enter the presence of the Lord. In the Book of Exodus, Moses was commanded by God to remove his sandals upon entering the holy ground surrounding the burning bush. Instant death was possible just for touching the Ark of the Covenant, when forbidden to do so. Even the high priest of Israel had to go through an extraordinarily elaborate preparation just to spend a few minutes inside the most sacred section of the temple called the Holy of Holies.

By the grace of God, things changed dramatically upon the arrival of our Immanuel, Jesus Christ. As the Messiah lived among the people, He actually invited sinners to come close to Him with no prerequisite ceremony. He allowed those who were considered unclean to touch the fringes of His robes. Therefore we too, though unworthy and imperfect in our own ways, join in this freedom to be able to boldly approach Him with confidence.

Through His sacrifice on the Cross, Jesus Christ has completely torn the veil whose job it was to set apart that which is holy from that which is profane. Indeed, for those who are saved, the Holy Spirit actually enters into our hearts (John 14:17). We no longer need to fear instant death when coming before the Lord - we are welcomed now as children of the Most High. But this new birthright does not preclude us from bestowing added homage to the Lord of Lords by approaching humbly and bowing before Him. Indeed, now as the redeemed and adopted children of God, our desire to more fully pursue praising Him should grow even greater, in response to His great love for us.

Postures of Praise

The genesis of this book came from taking a close examination of behaviors that are often overlooked or taken for granted, and the ideas within are meant to be a reflection on how we react when confronted with the presence of the Holy One. Why do we at times feel compelled to stand in worship, or to raise our hands? How did these gestures acquire the meanings associated with them? Do these actions come from an emotion in our hearts, one that we are unable to express through words alone? Though worshipping God in this physical way is not required of us, we see that the Bible is teeming with encouragement to use our bodies to glorify God.

Hopefully this kind of review could be a starting point to expand our perspective on what worship is, and lead us to examine the potential for what it could be. The point of this study is to encourage an approach to worship that is more deliberate and thoughtful, while still retaining joyful spontaneity. These pages contain no instruction, definition, or explanation of worship. Rather, this study is humbly shared to inspire and encourage all Christ-followers to further our own personal worship journeys.

The following chapters contain a selection of metaphors, analogies, stories, and pictures painted to highlight different aspects of the way that we approach worship. There is no limit to God's glory, and so our approach to showing love and adoration to Him should reflect that. We want to use every possible avenue to worship God, echoing the heart of King David, who said, "I will celebrate before the Lord. I will become even more undignified than this, and I will be humiliated in my own eyes" (2 Samuel 6:21-22, NIV).

These pictures are also an invitation to put time, energy, and thought into all of our expressions of worship. Our postures of praise may not have been waiting for an interpretation, but perhaps through examining them closer, we may find new joy in demonstrating holy adoration through our body worship. The glory of God is ever expanding - so let our understanding of worship ever expand as we dive deeper in proskuneo before the Lord.

Praise the Lord.
Praise God in his sanctuary;
praise him in his mighty heavens.
Praise him for his acts of power;
praise him for his surpassing greatness.
Praise him with the sounding of the trumpet,
praise him with the harp and lyre,
praise him with timbrel and dancing,
praise him with the strings and pipe,
praise him with the clash of cymbals,
praise him with resounding cymbals.
Let everything that has breath praise the Lord.
Praise the Lord.
(Psalms 150:1-6, NIV)

A JOYFUL NOISE

Clap your hands, all peoples!
Shout to God with loud songs of joy!
For the Lord, the Most High, is to be feared,
a great king over all the earth.
(Psalms 47:1-2, ESV)

Sprinkled throughout the Psalms is the command to clap our hands in worship - though this may not exactly fit the definition of a posture, it is nonetheless a physical action by which we can convey meaning and emotion. God delights in the joyful noise of His people, and clapping is one way of making sound that is second nature to humans. Babies do not need to be taught how to clap - it is something that they can do instinctively, as an expression of joy from an innocent heart. It is something that we do as adults as a particular form of communication, used as a way to express happiness or affirmation.

For example, whenever a powerful point is made during a speech, clapping can be heard throughout the assembled crowd. The audience use the clamor to convey to the speaker that they agree with what he or she is saying. And if the point really hits home, then the reaction can be so loud and sustained that the speaker may have trouble getting back to their speech, and may have to ask the gathering to settle down so that they can continue their address.

Clapping is a natural response to something great, and greatness can be found in an almost infinite number of areas. It could be a reaction to hearing a stirring musical performance, seeing an amazing physical feat at a sporting event, or even from watching a movie or play that has swept you up in the plot. If you are moved, if you are joyful, or if you just want to share your agreement without using words, you can clap your hands to communicate how you feel.

If clapping is a natural response to something great, then the question must be asked - who or what is greater than the true and living God? He is the center of the universe, and worthy of all praise - spoken and unspoken. We are called to worship Him with all the praises of our hearts, with singing, with musical instruments, and with a joyful noise. And the most elementary way to make noise is to clap your hands together – the most ancient of all percussion instruments.

Roar of the Crowd

One unique aspect about using clapping as part of our worship is that it can be communal -

there is power in a crowd clapping their hands to-gether. One person clapping by him or herself can at times be awkward, but get a group of people clap-ping together and it can make a deafening sound. Of course, there is the infamous 'slow-clap', where an individual in a group begins to cautiously clap alone - quiet, uneven, and slightly embarrassing at first, but then as others are inspired to join in, the noise quickly grows in power and intensity until it bursts like a storm cloud, with thunder and roar.

In our culture, the standing ovation is the highest form of communal clapping that ex-ists. Reflect on the many examples that we have seen throughout history, applied after a moving speech or a great performance of stage or sport. The word ovation is derived from the Latin word 'Ovatio' (from 'Ovare'), which means 'to rejoice'. Is that not the perfect word to describe the feeling when our hearts are bursting with praise for our God - we stand and rejoice in Him. Let us give our Lord a standing ovation, while singing praise to our Savior and King, for He is worthy, forever worthy!

The command in the Psalms to clap is not directed just at individuals, but rather to all peoples together. How many concerts or worship events have we been to where the sound of clapping some-how overtakes the sound of the drums and other instruments, even though the band is using high-powered amplifiers, loudspeakers, and other sound equipment designed to project music over the audi-ence. That is how we are called to respond to His glory, to make a joyful and loud noise!

Even the natural world around us is erupting in praise to the Lord, as it is written, "the mountains and hills will burst into song before you, and all the trees of the field will clap their hands" (Isaiah 55:12, NIV). We gladly join in with all of creation to declare that our Lord is the Most High, our great King worthy of all praise. Let us worship our God with a holy and joyful noise.

Make a joyful noise unto the Lord, all the earth: make a loud noise, and rejoice, and sing praise.
(Psalms 98:4, KJV)

EYES CLOSED

"What no eye has seen, what no ear has heard,
and what no human mind has conceived"
- the things God has prepared
for those who love him -
these are the things God has revealed
to us by his Spirit.
(1 Corinthians 2:9-10, NIV)

One of the most ubiquitous announcements during our modern church services is the request for the congregation to turn off their cell phones and other electronics, a message also commonly heard in other types of venues, such as movie theaters and playhouses. This petition is made in order to minimize outside interference and distractions during the service. In a similar vein, during times of prayer and worship we often close our eyes, in order to shift our focus away from the world around us. This helps us to concentrate on communing with God, and to experience all that we can from this sacred time.

Of course, the Holy Spirit is able to reach into our souls at any time and communicate directly with us, but during times set aside for prayer and worship, we close our eyes to hone in on God and raise our spiritual senses, so as to not miss out on anything that He might have for us. When a person loses one of their physical senses, such as hearing or sight, their other senses can often become heightened to make up for the loss – in a similar manner, we can close our eyes to make our hearts more sensitive to the Spirit. Here are a few examples to further illustrate the effect that closing our eyes can have in worship.

Meditation

Blessed is the one
who does not walk in step with the wicked
or stand in the way that sinners take
or sit in the company of mockers,
but whose delight is in the law of the Lord,
and who meditates on his law day and night.
(Psalms 1:1-2, NIV)

Meditation is not necessarily just a new-age practice, or discipline solely used by eastern religions; it is a technique that can be beneficial to anyone seeking to improve their concentration. This method of increasing focus on the current moment, by closing off your senses to all outside stimulation, can really help us to invest deeper in times of worship. Modern church services can sometimes rival elaborate rock concerts with flashing lights, high-definition video screens, and music blaring over the PA system. The overall effect can be very powerful and encouraging to the congregation, however some of the most meaningful times of worship can occur in moments of simple quiet, with hearts focused solely on the presence of the Lord.

Meditation can also help us to let go of our concerns by concentrating on the present, just as Jesus taught in the Sermon on the Mount. He encouraged the crowd, who had gathered to hear Him speak, that they should focus on following God's will in the moment, and to trust that God will take care of any struggles that they will face in the future. Jesus said, "seek first his kingdom and his righteousness, and all these things will be given to you as well. Therefore do not worry about tomorrow, for tomorrow will worry about itself. Each day has enough trouble of its own" (Matthew 6:34, NIV). We focus on being faithful in following God today, and He promises to provide what we need for tomorrow. And during times of hardship, when our lives can sometimes feel like a string of emergencies, one following another - even then we must not allow ourselves to be distracted from seeking God first and foremost.

About our daily needs, Jesus said, "Therefore I tell you, do not worry about your life, what you will eat or drink; or about your body, what you will wear. Is not life more than food, and the body more than clothes? Look at the birds of the air; they do not sow or reap or store away in barns, and yet your heavenly Father feeds them. Are you not much more valuable than they? Can any one of you by worrying add a single hour to your life?" (Matthew 6:25-27, NIV). The same day-to-day struggles and concerns that plagued ancient Jewish life continue to plague our modern world as well, in spite of all our social and technological advances. We still need to be reminded to trust that God is our source of all provision, and to remember that He is sufficient for us.

We are called to lay aside our cares and our worries, instead of using all of our energy to fight for every cent, every step, or every second of our lives. We must realign our priorities and not lose sight of the fact that no matter how difficult our situation may be, there is nothing that God Almighty cannot do. That is the challenge of faith, to put our hope in the Lord alone, and trust in His promises to provide for us.

We are people of the Sabbath - called to rest and leave behind our stress and worries in a way that displays our faith in God, because He alone is Jehovah Jireh, the great provider. We are not so naive as to think that we have no part to play in whether we eat or drink - but beyond our present reality, we know that it is truly God who holds our lives in His hands. We can trust in our good Father to sustain us, and to bestow upon us all that we need, according to His grace and will.

As we praise the true and living God, let us close our eyes and meditate on the Biblical truths implanted in the songs we sing. The challenge is to "Set your minds on things above, not on earthly things" (Colossians 3:2, NIV). Let the teachings of Scripture root themselves in our hearts where they will continue to grow and blossom in our lives. Let us focus on the presence of the Holy Spirit, and may the world around us grow dim as the light of God grows brighter.

Surprise

Every good and perfect gift is from above,
coming down from the Father of the heavenly lights
(James 1:17, NIV)

Is there more satisfaction in receiving a gift, or in giving a gift? Getting a present, whether for your birthday, Christmas, or any other occasion, always feels good - it makes you feel special and loved. But isn't there greater joy in giving a gift to a friend or family member? Don't you love the process of searching for the perfect gift, wrapping it in paper, and then finally giving it to that special person? And sweet is the reward, to see the look of surprise and gratitude in their eyes, when the present is exactly what they wanted. The Book of Acts makes it clear what side we are to be on as Christians, as it is written, "In everything I did, I showed you that by this kind of hard work we must help the weak, remembering the words the Lord Jesus himself said: 'It is more blessed to give than to receive'" (Acts 20:35, NIV).

Giving presents is an act of affection that

many people enjoy - we desire to give good gifts to the special people in our lives. They are often covered in wrapping paper to hide what is inside, which allows us to watch the faces of our loved ones as they tear off the coverings, and to see the pure delight in receiving that perfect present. Sometimes the gift can be too large to cover in gift wrap, and in those instances we make the recipient keep their eyes closed, to hold in the feeling of surprise until the big reveal.

Similarly, that same feeling of joyous excitement can happen outside of physical gift-giving. For unexpected birthday parties or family reunions, such as military homecomings, friends and family will often keep their loved one's eyes covered, in order to maintain the suspense and anticipation. How happy we are when someone close to us has gone to great lengths to prepare a special gift or event; but isn't it true that the happiest people are really the ones preparing the surprise? At the moment everything is revealed, the giver knows exactly what is about to happen, except for how the recipient will react, and they can hardly contain their joy.

Just like earthly parents preparing the perfect presents for their children, our Heavenly Father is eager to give us all that we need, as it is written, "God will supply all your needs according to His riches in glory in Christ Jesus" (Philippians 4:19, NASB). God has so much in store for us, and all we have to do is bring our requests to Him. As Jesus said, "Ask and it will be given to you; seek and you will find; knock and the door will be opened to you. For everyone who asks receives; the one who seeks finds; and to the one who knocks, the door will be opened" (Matthew 7:7-8, NIV).

There is no limit to the love of our Heavenly Father, and no limit to what He will give us, which He unequivocally proved through the sacrifice of Jesus Christ. "He who did not spare his own Son, but gave him up for us all - how will he not also, along with him, graciously give us all things?" (Romans 8:32, NIV). It is exceedingly rare for a man to die for someone else, but next to impossible to imagine a father letting his own precious son die for another. Yet that is precisely the impossible kind of love that God has for us. "This is love: not that we loved God, but that he loved us and sent his Son as an atoning sacrifice for our sins" (1 John 4:10, NIV). No request we have could ever be costlier than what God has already given for us. He is our good Father, and we are His adopted children – in comparison to even the most loving and generous human parents, "how much more will your Father in heaven give good gifts to those who ask him!" (Matthew 7:11, NIV).

During our times of worship, God is so eager to pour out His blessings over us. He gives us gifts of encouragement, love, truth, grace, mercy, kindness, forgiveness, and so much more - all we need to do is open our hearts to receive. How many life-changing revelations or affirmations have occurred in our own lives, as we have offered songs of praise to our Lord? We cry out for more, knowing that there is no end to the grace God gives to us.

As we sing, let us close our eyes in worship, in joyful anticipation of the gifts we are about to receive. We do not know what God has prepared for us when we approach the Mercy Seat, so let us close our eyes in excitement and expectancy, knowing that as we ask more from Him, our Father will not hold back from us. He may answer in ways that we could not have imagined, or would not have chosen otherwise - therefore we blindly approach in faith, seeking His kingdom first, and knowing that all that we need will be given to us according to His will.

We close our eyes in faith, knowing that our God is with us, and we can hold on to Him alone. We do not know what He has in store for us in worship - joy, encouragement, or perhaps even a rebuke or a call to repentance, to return to a clean heart. Whatever He gives to us, we know it will be for our good. Trusting in our Lord, we enter worship with our eyes closed, eager to receive the gifts our Father has prepared for us.

Kiss

Let him kiss me with the kisses of his mouth!
For your love is better than wine
(Song of Solomon 1:2, ESV)

A romantic kiss is more than just the mere touching of lips. A kiss can be powerful - indeed, many folk stories from around the world have assigned an almost magical power to the act, such as the kiss that broke Sleeping Beauty's curse. Health researchers have expounded in great detail all of the health benefits from kissing, which they say can lower stress and increase production of hormones associated with feeling happy. Kissing has been a part of human life for millennia, and has been recorded as such in some of the earliest written sources in history.

A kiss can happen in the middle of a crowded room, yet for the couple entwined, they could for that moment be the only two people on Earth. Wedding ceremonies prominently feature a first kiss, after the man and wife have been declared officially married. And the 'Kiss Cam' is always a crowd favorite when going to American sporting events, guaranteed to make you smile or laugh. Put simply, kissing is a special connection between two people in love, and in our culture, when leaning in for a kiss, couples close their eyes and embrace.

Why do we close our eyes when we kiss? Is this some kind of instinct to protect our eyes, like a reflex? Or is it something more than that? Think back to your first kiss, and remember how many thoughts and emotions were racing back and forth in your mind. If you were like me, you were probably thinking something like: "Is now the right moment? Should I lean in? Does she want me to kiss her? Oh, whatever, just go for it!"

In that magical moment, there is so much anticipation that it can feel like time is actually slowing down – we are filled with so much hope and excitement, while at the same time facing uncertainty and the fear of rejection. Our hearts are pounding, cheeks are flushed red, we're breathing hard - and in that moment our eyes seem to close by themselves. It is such an intimate act, one that binds us physically and emotionally to this other person, that we cannot help but be overwhelmed by it.

Kissing is a physically intimate act, one in which we connect with another person by inviting them close to ourselves. In a similar vein, worship is a spiritually intimate act, one in which we connect with God and invite Him to enter into the deepest places of our souls. It binds us, though we are mortal and imperfect, to our Holy Creator. It is easy to feel overwhelmed in moments of true worship - indeed, is this not to be expected? One does not simply walk into the presence of the Divine and walk out without being changed.

Fearfully we approach the throne, knowing that we are unworthy, and with hearts pounding we find that instead of rejection, we receive acceptance. Instead of judgement, we receive mercy. Instead of being cast out, we are adopted as His own. Like a righteous cancer, holiness attacks our sinful hearts and spreads throughout our whole being, transforming us to be more like the Holy One.

Therefore, is it not natural to feel overwhelmed and close our eyes in worship, just as we do when we kiss? As we open ourselves to the Lord, we know there is nothing that we can hide behind, as the Bible says, "Nothing in all creation is hidden from God's sight. Everything is uncovered and laid bare before the eyes of him to whom we must give account" (Hebrews 4:13, NIV).

As impossible as it would be to try to hide our physical flaws when getting close enough to kiss someone, how impossible would it be to try to hide our spiritual flaws as we come close to God? But this is not a reason to shy away, as God embraces the one who repents before Him. As the Samaritan woman at the well would encourage us, "'Come, see a man who told me everything I ever did. Could this be the Messiah?'" (John 4:29, NIV). Jesus laid out all the ways that this woman had sinned in her life, but instead of running away, she fully embraced forgiveness and the new beginning that the Savior offered to her.

This Christ knows us - He knows everything we have ever done, and yet still loves us as we are, with true unconditional love. And we worship Him for who He was, is, and always will be. He leans in to us, inviting us, embracing us, and we can trust that He will always love and protect us. No flaw, no sin, no accusation, no temptation, or anything else could ever drive a wedge between God and His beloved. As the Apostle Paul writes, "For I am convinced that neither death nor life, neither angels nor demons, neither the present nor the future, nor any powers, neither height nor depth, nor anything else in all creation, will be able to separate us from the love of God that is in Christ Jesus our Lord" (Romans

8:38-39, NIV). In response to this overwhelming love, let us lean in to experience this bond with the Lord, let us fall into His embrace, and close our eyes in intimate worship with our God.

I pray that the eyes of your heart
may be enlightened in order
that you may know the hope
to which he has called you,
the riches of his glorious inheritance
in his holy people,
and his incomparably great power
for us who believe.
(Ephesians 1:18-19, NIV)

RISE

Stand up and praise the Lord your God,
who is from everlasting to everlasting.
(Nehemiah 9:5, NIV)

The simple act of standing can be powerful
- think back to the iconic image of the anonymous
'Tank Man' during the Tiananmen Square Protests,
standing alone in front of a line of military tanks
and preventing their advance. In April 1989, large
student-led demonstrations broke out across China,
demanding reforms from the communist government, and ultimately culminating in a huge gathering at Tiananmen Square in central Beijing. For
months, these demonstrators peacefully challenged
their nation's leadership for reforms to what they
saw as a broken and corrupt system, with many
even going on hunger strikes to add urgency to
their movement. Parts of the Chinese government
wavered between opening up a dialogue with the
demonstrators and cracking down on them, but ultimately a peaceful resolution was never reached.
At the beginning of June, the government decided

to send the military and police to clear the square and forcibly end the protests, leading to violence, arrests, and the deaths of an undetermined number of people, with some reports estimating casualties to be in the thousands.

On June 5th of that year, a scene unfolded in the midst of the chaos that caught the attention of news photographers, one of whom captured the defining picture from the demonstrations and the crackdown that followed. A column of tanks was moving in the northeast corner of Tiananmen Square down a wide boulevard, when a lone man, dressed just like any other ordinary citizen and carrying a couple of shopping bags, simply walked into the middle of the street. He stood directly in front of the lead tank to block its progress, and forced the entire column to grind to a halt. The lead tank then tried to drive around the man, but the protester deftly moved with the tank to continuously block it, and as the tank commander was presumably unwilling to run the man over, there was nothing left to do but for the armored vehicles to come to a complete and reluctant stop.

This lone nameless man, his bravery forever captured in the famous photograph, risked his life in the moment, as well as in the aftermath of the crackdown, to protect those who would never know who he was, and in the process has inspired countless others to stand against injustice. One frail human body with no protection, standing in defiance of fear, and forcing tons of armored vehicles to come to an unwilling halt - an amazing story, with the most unlikely of heroes. What a display of selfless sacrifice, one without the possibility of any self-benefit - an illustration of the power that comes from the simple act of standing up, and an example that we as Christians could learn so much from. This chapter offers several pictures of the call to stand in our culture that can be applied to our hearts when we rise to worship God.

Standing Room Only

My foot stands on level ground;
in the great assembly I will bless the Lord.
(Psalms 26:12, ESV)

Attending sporting events is one of the most popular activities in our culture today. Going to the ballpark can be a treat for a special occasion, or it can be part of a time-honored family tradition. In many ways, sports can mirror the human experience - for example, football has often been compared to war as the two teams battle each other for territory. Even the Bible frequently uses sports as a metaphor for life, such as in the Book of Hebrews, where the author encourages believers to "run with perseverance the race marked out for us, fixing our eyes on Jesus, the pioneer and perfecter of faith" (Hebrews 12:1-2, NIV). This passage compares life to a marathon, with the goal being to push ourselves as hard as we can to claim the prize set before us.

So how are sports related to our modern worship experience? Consider the way that stadiums and sports arenas in our current era are designed, with the inner-most sacred space of the playing field being set apart for only certain designated persons, such as players, coaches, and officials. This central area is then surrounded by rows and rows of seats, each with different levels of accessibility based upon status or cost of admission - a design feature that can be traced back to antiquity, with the way that structures like the Colosseum of Ancient Rome were built. Today's arenas have courtside seats and luxury boxes for those who can afford it, and cheap seats for those who cannot - the Colosseum had boxes as well, reserved for the Emperor and other high-ranking officials. Roman senators had seating available to them along the same level, with non-senatorial nobles right behind. Further away from the arena floor were levels for ordinary citizens, with the wealthy being able to sit closer to the action, separated from the common plebeians. And at the very top was the highest level, where all the other spectators strained their eyes to see the action, including the poor and slaves; this level was perhaps without seating altogether.

With stadiums of today, for important events there can be countless people wanting to enter, but those without tickets are not allowed into the building at all. Only the lucky few with the right passes can enter, but if the tickets they have were cheaply purchased, then the closest they can get to are the seats furthest from the game action. These levels are satirically described as nosebleed sections, the joke being that they are located so high above the field, that sitting there might cause altitude sickness. Those with more expensive tickets are allowed closer to the playing field, but even they are restricted from ever getting onto the field itself, no matter how exorbitant the amount paid.

Coaches are allowed on the sidelines, from where they can command the actions of their players, but even they cannot be on the field while the game is in play. Then there are the reserve players who are good enough to be on the team, and might actually see some game action if the opportunity arises, but for the most part are just relegated to waiting on the bench, which is why they are nicknamed 'benchwarmers'. It is only the best of the best of the players who are allowed onto the field itself, at the center of the stadium, with all eyes on them.

These zones of access in stadiums not only control who can go where, but they are also very effective in passively reminding attendees of their own social worth and standing. The location of your seat is an unmistakable status symbol, by which the wealthy and powerful can literally turn their backs on the crowd behind them. Benchwarmers cannot escape the fact that they are not as athletically talented as those allowed to play the entire game. Those sitting in the nosebleed sections cannot help but stare jealously at the backs of those who can afford the more expensive seats. Inequality is constructed into the very design of the building itself, reminding everyone who enters that there is little fairness in our fallen world - there has always been those with more, and those with less. This segregation based on access to different levels is very reminiscent of the way that the temple of God was built in the Old Testament.

In the temple, there were curtains, walls, and courtyards creating zones of separation to remind the people of their place in society, based on the areas they had access to. There were people who were forbidden from even entering the temple walls itself, and had to remain outside, such as lepers. There was a courtyard for foreigners and for women. There was a more centrally located courtyard for Jewish males of good social and religious standing. Then there was the inner portion where only priests could enter, and finally the special room at the very heart of the complex named the Holy of Holies, which was separated from everything else by a thick veil. That was where the Lord would appear as a cloud over the Mercy Seat, which was atop the Ark of the Covenant. Into this Most Holy Place no human other than the high priest could enter, and even he was allowed to enter only during the High Holy Day of Yom Kippur, the Day of Atonement, the holiest day of the Jewish calendar. But no matter what level of access they had to the complex, every person entering the temple would invariably set their eyes on the central area, where all of the important actions were taking place, just as every chair in a modern arena is perfectly oriented towards the center of the playing field.

Stadiums are also built in such a way so as to provide the best viewing opportunity from every seat, from the plush expensive armchairs close to the field, to the bare metal benches in the top levels. The rows of seating rise sharply from the floor of the arena all the way almost to the ceiling, and are arranged in such a way that spectators can comfortably see all of the action even while seated, the steep angle providing a way for people to look over the heads of those in front of them. Some movie theaters are even constructed in this way, with angled rows of seats rising vertically behind each other, and this design is referred to as stadium seating. Those who are of shorter stature do not have to worry about being seated behind taller people, and no one ever has to stand to get a good view of the game.

But what happens during the most crucial, game-changing moments of action? In the bottom of the ninth inning, bases loaded with two outs, and the home team's slugger hits a long fly ball - what do you do, in expectation of greatness? You rise. Or in overtime, on fourth down, with the game on the line, and the quarterback throws up a Hail Mary pass to the endzone - what do you do, in expectation of greatness? You rise from your seat. Or in stoppage time, at the end of the match, and your side has one penalty kick left to win it all - what do you do, in expectation of greatness? You rise to your feet.

When it matters the most, regardless of

where they are seated, all of the fans in the stadium will rise to their feet as one, and it is not to get a better view. They get up on their feet in anticipation, in expectation of greatness - they know something amazing is coming and they do not want to miss one second of it. They do not need to stand to see over the person in front of them, and they don't care about blocking the person behind them - they rise in excitement, to witness something that they will remember long after the game ends. It doesn't matter if they are just a few feet away from the action or in the furthest section - no matter where they are, fans are compelled to get on their feet. Even those watching the game from home on their televisions will stand, which obviously has nothing to do with trying to get a better view, but still they rise, hoping to see something amazing.

What a wonderful analogy for the people of God, as we rise to our feet during worship - though the congregation could enjoy singing praise songs while seated just as easily as they could while standing, we are compelled to stand because we do not want to miss a second of what God has in store for us. Every moment of worship is precious and exciting, and we want to witness the way the Holy Spirit moves as we praise the Lord. We don't need to stand to see over the person in front of us, and we don't care about blocking the person behind us - we are simply excited and desperate to see what God will do.

Seat location does not matter - if the Spirit

is moving, then we are as close as we can be, right from where we are. The veil has been torn, the Holy of Holies has been thrown open, the Holy Spirit has been let loose in our hearts, and we the redeemed are now allowed free entry into the very presence of God. There are no longer any zones designating who is important and who is not; for believers, there is no separation between those with access and those without. Indeed, the Book of Revelation tells us that in Heaven there will not even be a temple, describing paradise as having "no temple in the city, for its temple is the Lord God the Almighty and the Lamb" (Revelation 21:22, ESV).

We all are now a part of the action, no longer apart from the action. We can now go where it was formerly forbidden, as the Bible announces, "Therefore, brothers and sisters, since we have confidence to enter the Most Holy Place by the blood of Jesus, by a new and living way opened for us through the curtain, that is, his body, and since we have a great priest over the house of God, let us draw near to God with a sincere heart and with the full assurance that faith brings, having our hearts sprinkled to cleanse us from a guilty conscience and having our bodies washed with pure water" (Hebrews 10:19-22, NIV). God isn't looking for only the best of the best, instead He invites everyone in as full participants - there are no benchwarmers in the Kingdom of Heaven.

All are welcome to join the Great Banquet that Jesus described in a parable, "A man once gave a great banquet and invited many. And at the time for the banquet he sent his servant to say to those who had been invited, 'Come, for everything is now ready'" (Luke 14:16-17, ESV). What happens next was completely unexpected, as all of the invited guests inexplicably begin to make excuses as to why they could not attend.

The man throwing the banquet then does something equally unexpected – instead of cancelling the event, he decides to go through with the dinner, and seeks to fill his house by bringing in those who would have otherwise felt unworthy to enter. The man told his servant, "'Go out quickly to the streets and lanes of the city, and bring in the poor and crippled and blind and lame.' And the servant said, 'Sir, what you commanded has been done, and still there is room.' And the master said to the servant, 'Go out to the highways and hedges and compel people to come in, that my house may be filled'" (Luke 14:21-23, ESV).

This is the evangelistic heart of God, that He opens wide the doors to His Kingdom and seeks to fill it with those who the world would rate as unworthy. Hallelujah, that there is room for us, and even now He is compelling more and more souls to come to the feast. Heaven is not just for the rich and powerful to enjoy, and for the outcasts to view from outside. In utter contrast with the way that the world assigns status and worth to people, Jesus tells us that in His kingdom, "the last will be first, and the first will be last" (Matthew 20:16, NIV).

We are all invited to the feast as equal recipients of grace. All are welcomed in as His banquet guests. In response to this invitation, "Let us then approach God's throne of grace with confidence, so that we may receive mercy and find grace to help us in our time of need" (Hebrews 4:16, NIV).

As we live here on Earth, we may still have our own personal races to run, but we know that the contest between good and evil has already been decided, and that our Lord is the ultimate champion - His victory has been sealed for all eternity. So let the people of God arise, more enthusiastic than even the most fanatic of sports fans, dressed not in imitation team jerseys, but rather "clothed in white robes, with palm branches in their hands, and crying out with a loud voice, 'Salvation belongs to our God who sits on the throne, and to the Lamb!'" (Revelation 7:9-10, ESV).

Our God is not done yet, and He is still moving in miraculous ways, we can be sure of that. Let us stand in gratitude of being invited into the Kingdom, in anticipation of great works, and in fervent expectation of the amazing. Desperately awaiting to see what God has next for us and for our world, let us stand and worship Him.

On any given Sunday morning, as we walk into service as the music plays, and we invite God to come into our worship - what do you do, in expectation of greatness? You rise to your feet. Does it really matter what song the band starts playing, which pastor is giving the sermon, or if your friends saved you a seat? When God enters, we know that great things are bound to happen. Therefore, let us rise in expectation of the greatness to come. Let us stand and worship our Lord.

All Rise

For the Lord is our judge,
the Lord is our lawgiver,
the Lord is our king;
it is he who will save us.
(Isaiah 33:22, NIV)

The courtroom is a place where justice is sought and judgement is delivered. The very name reflects the royal heritage associated with its role in society, as historically it was in a king's court where legal cases were decided. Recall the story of King Solomon (1 Kings 3:16-28), where he is asked to judge between two mothers, each claiming a single baby boy as their own. Unable to determine who was speaking the truth and who was lying, Solomon called for a sword in order for the baby to be split in two, so that the claimants could each have a half. One woman was satisfied with his pronouncement, as she wickedly thought that if she could not have the child for herself, then neither should her rival. But the true mother revealed herself when she renounced her claim, begging Solomon to change his ruling and instead give her son to the lying woman, as she would rather have her child alive with another mother than have the baby die. The people of Israel took this case as a sign of the great wisdom that had been bestowed on Solomon, and they put their trust in his judgements. At that time, and for much of human history, there was no higher judge than the king of the land.

The legal system of today has been greatly expanded, and in many ways the modern American trial is like a playhouse drama, one of them is that there is a cast of characters involved, each with a specific role. The main character at the center of all the action is the judge. The judge holds power over all of the other characters - no matter how important or powerful they may be out in the world, inside the courtroom the judge is completely in charge. The words that come from the judge's mouth are binding, and their decisions must be followed without exception - their decrees become the law itself, which we see in the legal principles of precedent and stare decisis. The judge has at their discretion judgement and wrath, punishment and conviction, or mercy and grace.

There are other characters in the drama as well, adding nuance to every case. They each have their own parts to play: defense attorneys, prosecutors, defendants and plaintiffs, members of the jury, law enforcement, clerks and stenographers, and the friends and families of those involved. They all have their own roles, they may speak at times, they may even lead the judge towards one side or the other - but at the end of the day, it is the judge who makes the ultimate decision in any trial.

The American courtroom has been the setting for countless movies and television shows. Through these fictionalized depictions, the customs and procedures in legal proceedings have seeped into our collective understanding, becoming familiar to all, even those who may have never stepped foot inside a courtroom before. The chamber's layout is instantly recognizable; there is a seating section for the audience, desks for the lawyers, a box for the jury to sit in, and a raised platform at center-stage for the judge. Jurists today will refer to their seat as the bench, as historically they used to sit upon actual benches, perhaps with other magistrates to preside over cases together. Lawyers may at times be instructed to approach the bench to confer privately with the judge during a trial.

There is an order to events for every court proceeding, and all in attendance must adhere to that schedule. The drama begins with setting the scene: clerks will come into the courtroom to prepare the necessary paperwork, and members of the public will file into the gallery. Then the lawyers will begin to enter, along with witnesses, plaintiffs, and then the defendants involved in the case. The jury may at that time be summoned from their meeting room, and seated along the side of the room. The stage has now been set for the most important character to make their entrance.

At the appropriate time, the hallway doors will close and no one else will be allowed in. A hush falls over the gathered audience, almost like the moment in a theater right before the curtain lifts. Then the bailiff steps to the front to speak, and with the utmost formality, this officer of the law announces the arrival of the judge. They give the command that sets the entire drama into motion with the simple phrase, "All rise." At that moment, no matter what role they play in the trial, everyone stands. It doesn't matter who they are outside of that room, rich or poor, powerful or weak - all who are in the courtroom must rise to their feet.

Finally, the judge enters the chamber, with the entire audience standing in silence, in deference to the judicial office. And everyone remains on their feet, until the judge sits and releases them from this duty, and allows them to take their seats again. But what is the purpose of this command to rise? And at what point in history did it become a custom? Undoubtedly it would be unlawful not to follow the order to rise if physically able, and one would risk the wrath of the court and punishment for failing to comply. Nevertheless, it is a fascinating tradition that has become standard in courthouses around the world.

It does not matter if the audience knows the judge personally, or if they are familiar with past judgements or other work. It does not matter if the judge has been serving in this role for many years, or is sitting for his or her first case. Everyone in the courtroom stands out of respect, simply to honor the position that the judge holds. Indeed, even the way that judges are addressed as 'Your Honor' reflects the high esteem their profession deserves.

Whether the audience agrees with the coming verdict or not, all must stand. Whether innocent or guilty, the accused must stand. Whether the lawyers are prosecuting or defending, they must stand. Everyone knows that the judge rules over all aspects in that room, and therefore they honor him by getting on their feet. Outside of the courthouse the judge may be just another anonymous human being, but in the courtroom the judge is a symbol of justice itself, the hope that all humanity shares - that in the end, evil will be punished and truth will be victorious.

If we stand to honor a human judge, what then shall we do in worship, when the eternal Judge, God Himself, enters the room? Common among the different Christian traditions throughout the world is the call to stand as worship services begin, and there are many parallels between standing to honor the Lord and standing when a judge enters court. One day, whether they believe in Christ as their Savior or not, all of mankind will have to stand in the heavenly courtroom and be judged, as it is written, "For we must all appear before the judgment seat of Christ, so that each of us may receive what is due us for the things done while in the body, whether good or bad" (2 Corinthians 5:10, NIV).

We stand, whether we are guilty or innocent. We stand, whether we have been faithfully worshipping for many years, or if this is the first time we recognize the Lord as our God. We stand, whether we are the ones singing, or the ones being sung over. It is an act of worship to stand in honor and deference to the one true Judge of the universe, because by rising to our feet, we recognize His authority over the entire universe.

The Bible is full of references to God in His role as the ultimate Judge. "He calls to the heavens above and to the earth, that he may judge his people: 'Gather to me my faithful ones, who made a covenant with me by sacrifice!' The heavens declare his righteousness, for God himself is judge!" (Psalms 50:4-6, NIV). Those who break earthly laws must face earthly judges, but those who break God's law will be judged by God himself. There is no one who can escape the coming judgement, for "All who sin apart from the law will also perish apart from the law, and all who sin under the law will be judged by the law" (Romans 2:12, NIV).

There is no higher court to appeal to, for the judgement of God is final. "There is only one Lawgiver and Judge, the one who is able to save and destroy" (James 4:12, NIV). It was God who created the law by which all of mankind will be judged. He has examined our hearts and our souls, and has found us to be guilty, as the Book of Romans explains, "for all have sinned and fall short of the glory of God" (Romans 3:23, NIV).

We may try to hide or justify our own personal sinful nature, and rebel against God's authority. But in truth, we know that we are deserving of punishment for the evil in our hearts. As the Psalmist wrote, "For I know my transgressions, and my sin is always before me. Against you, you only, have I sinned and done what is evil in your sight; so you are right in your verdict and justified when you judge" (Psalms 51:3-4, NIV).

But in a twist that sets the Christian faith apart from every other religion or system of philosophy, God ruled us guilty, and then suffered the consequences Himself - somehow the Judge became the condemned. "'He himself bore our sins' in his body on the cross, so that we might die to sins and live for righteousness; 'by his wounds you have been healed'" (1 Peter 2:24, NIV). Jesus Christ took our punishment upon himself, though He was guiltless.

Once we were guilty, now we are innocent. Once we were doomed to die, now we have eternal life. "When you were dead in your sins and in the uncircumcision of your flesh, God made you alive with Christ. He forgave us all our sins, having canceled the charge of our legal indebtedness, which stood against us and condemned us; he has taken it away, nailing it to the cross" (Colossians 2:13-14, NIV).

The smoking fire pot and the flaming torch have both passed through (Genesis 15:17), and the punishment meant for man was instead taken by the Lamb of God. The covenant between God and those who believe in Him means that we can now lay claim to an innocence not our own. All that is needed is for us to accept Jesus as our Savior, as

"This righteousness is given through faith in Jesus Christ to all who believe" (Romans 3:22, NIV). There is no other path to salvation, as Jesus said, "I am the way and the truth and the life. No one comes to the Father except through me" (John 14:6, NIV).

Rather than fear His judgement, we know that the price has already been paid by the sacrifice that our Savior made on the Cross, as "the blood of Jesus his Son cleanses us from all sin" (1 John 1:7, ESV). Therefore, it would be unjust to condemn us now, as Christ has already received the full punishment on our behalf. And we know that to be unjust is categorically not in God's nature, as the Bible makes clear: "If we confess our sins, he is faithful and just to forgive us our sins and to cleanse us from all unrighteousness" (1 John 1:9, ESV).

God is the faithful judge, and we can be confident that He will set all things right, according to His will. There is no corruption in Him, no weakness, bias, or prejudice. Those who cry out for mercy will receive it, but those who hold on to sin and reject the free gift of salvation will be punished, as the Torah reminds us, "The Lord is slow to anger and abounding in steadfast love, forgiving iniquity and transgression, but he will by no means clear the guilty" (Numbers 14:18, ESV).

God is the supernatural Judge - the solemn black robes worn by human judges emphasize the serious nature of their role, unyielding in their commitment to carry out justice. The Lord has robes as well, though their color and proportion are beyond what words could fully capture. The Bible describes Him as having "the appearance of jasper and carnelian, and around the throne was a rainbow that had the appearance of an emerald" (Revelation 4:3, ESV). This Judge does not sit on a bench as earthly jurists do, but rather upon a heavenly dais, as the prophet Isaiah describes Him, "sitting upon a throne, high and lifted up; and the train of his robe filled the temple" (Isaiah 6:1, ESV). Even His robes are on a different scale than the robes of earthly judges, demonstrating that His power cannot be measured in human terms.

God is the very embodiment of justice, presiding over all of creation, and ensuring that light will be victorious over the darkness. We cry out to Him for true judgement, to return the universe back to the way it was supposed to be - we cry out for "your kingdom come, your will be done, on earth as it is in heaven" (Matthew 6:10, NIV). When the Judge of Heaven and Earth enters in, all must rise. We, as recipients of His mercy, will stand to praise Him for His judgement, which is just and gracious. So in our worship today, let all rise to honor the God of justice; let us rise to worship the Lord.

Here Comes the Bride

Hallelujah!
For the Lord our God the Almighty reigns.
Let us rejoice and exult and give him the glory,
for the marriage of the Lamb has come,

and his Bride has made herself ready.
(Revelation 19:6-7, ESV)

Other than the day of birth or death, is there a more important day in a person's life than the day of their wedding? The day when a man will "be united to his wife, and the two will become one flesh" (Matthew 19:5, NIV). Holy matrimony - it is a beautiful, sacred event, and one of the most important and cherished milestones along the journey of life. The concept of marriage is so significant and rich with meaning that nuptial imagery can be found throughout the Bible as an analogy used to describe God's love and commitment to His people.

The wedding ceremony has been celebrated throughout all of human history. In our modern society, it is one of the few remaining ceremonies that we still somewhat regularly attend. Other examples of ceremonies are graduations, baptisms, funerals, and perhaps even birthday celebrations. Even grander examples of ceremonies include presidential inaugurations or royal coronations.

Ceremonies are full of rituals that have deep meanings, a series of actions performed in a specific way that is shared within a culture. One example that the world looks forward to every few years are the opening ceremonies of the Olympic Games, which always includes the ritual of the Olympic torch being lit, symbolizing the ageless tradition of the games, and comradery (or competition) between nations. Every host country plans a new and unique interpretation of the lighting ritual, but the basic foundation never changes, and so it connects the ceremony with all those performed in the past.

Few ceremonies can rival weddings in terms of the symbolic nature of the rituals contained within, regardless of the background or traditions of the families involved. Some weddings will bring together people from different cultures, and become an opportunity for each side to experience customs from other parts of the world, offering insight into their new in-laws and the heritage they are now connected with. One ritual that can be found in Mexico is for the newlyweds to be entwined in 'El Lazo', a rope laid out like an infinity symbol over their shoulders, to symbolize that their marriage will last for eternity. Another example comes from the Congolese culture, in which new couples are forbidden from smiling on their wedding day, in order to symbolize just how serious they are about the marriage.

Jewish wedding ceremonies incorporate the ritual of erecting a canopy over the bride and groom, called a Chuppah, which is a sheet of cloth hung over four poles. It symbolizes the home that the new couple will build together, and signifies an open home with no walls, to display their commitment to hospitality. The canopy also represents a dwelling devoid of any furniture or possessions, to remind the couple that their home is not made up of the material things they will fill it up with, but that the true essence of any home is the family who lives there.

But even deeper than that, the Chuppah represents the very presence of God Himself, hovering over the couple, reminiscent of the pillar of cloud by day and pillar of fire by night that led the ancient Israelites through their journey in the wilderness and inhabited their place of worship. "By day the Lord went ahead of them in a pillar of cloud to guide them on their way and by night in a pillar of fire to give them light, so that they could travel by day or night. Neither the pillar of cloud by day nor the pillar of fire by night left its place in front of the people" (Exodus 13:21-22, NIV).

Jewish rabbis refer to this presence as the Shekhinah Glory of God, a physical and visible revelation of the Almighty, this pillar that traveled with the nation of Israel through the desert to the Promised Land. These were people who were newly freed from slavery in Egypt after hundreds of years of bondage, during which time doubt must have grown in their hearts regarding the promises that God had made to their father Abraham. With their sudden freedom, it must have been a revelation that God had finally turned His eyes upon them, and felt compassion for them. And as a caring Father, He led them by hand on their trek home, for forty years - a special grace allotted to His chosen people to remove all doubt of His existence and of His faithfulness to them.

During the journey out of Egypt to the land promised to Abraham, the Lord commanded Moses to create the tabernacle, a movable tent of worship built to His exact specifications. Once it was ready and prepared precisely as God had ordered, the Shekhinah presence descended upon it. "Then the cloud covered the tent of meeting, and the glory of the Lord filled the tabernacle. Moses could not enter the tent of meeting because the cloud had settled on it, and the glory of the Lord filled the tabernacle" (Exodus 40:34-35, NIV). The only response that the Israelites could have given to this amazing sight was to stand and worship from where they were. "Whenever the people saw the pillar of cloud standing at the entrance to the tent, they all stood and worshiped, each at the entrance to their tent" (Exodus 33:10, NIV).

Once the nation of Israel had finally arrived at the Promised Land, and later established Jerusalem as the holy city and as the location for the Temple of God, this Shekhinah Glory rested over the people, as a reminder of the protection and blessings that God had promised to them. The Bible refers to this covering cloud as a canopy, as in the Book of Isaiah: "Then the Lord will create over the whole site of Mount Zion and over her assemblies a cloud by day, and smoke and the shining of a flaming fire by night; for over all the glory there will be a canopy. There will be a booth for shade by day from the heat, and for a refuge and a shelter from the storm and rain" (Isaiah 4:5-6, ESV).

The nation of Israel knew that God was present whenever they saw the cloud hover over them. So, to this day, Jewish weddings will invoke this same imagery by using the Chuppah during the ceremony. This canopy symbolizes the very presence of God, hovering over the couple to be wed, reminding them of His promises, and protecting those under its shadow. What a beautiful representation of how God blesses the covenant of marriage as the new family is created, to be led by His presence through their own personal journey of life together.

American weddings also have rituals; for example there is the lighting of unity candles, having children involved as ring boys and flower girls, bouquet tossing, and throwing rice at the couple as they leave the chapel. Even having the newlyweds feed each other the wedding cake is an example of a ritual embedded in marriage ceremonies, although typically the cake is eaten after the actual ceremony is finished. These rituals reveal aspects of our culture that have been carried on for hundreds of years, perhaps having lost their original meaning, but still retained as tradition. For example, throwing rice today may seem like a strange convention, but it is symbolic for wishing the new couple prosperity. In the rural society from which this tradition began, having a lot of grain meant food security and wealth, so wedding guests would shower the bride and groom with rice to wish them plenty of both.

Today, preparation for the actual wedding ceremony can take a long time, as everything has to be perfect for the big day. Every detail is important, because for the happy couple, the memories of this day will last for the rest of their lives, as the first day of their new lives together. Typically, a wedding will be the most lavish celebration a family will ever have, so both the groom's side and the bride's side will offer the very best that they can, to ensure that their guests have a wonderful time as they celebrate the joyful union. The newlyweds are surrounded and feted by family, friends, and loved ones from all over - invitees are often happy to spend large amounts of money on travel and lodging just to attend the ceremony.

On no other day is a woman more photographed than on her wedding day, in an effort to capture her image at the height of physical beauty. So finding the perfect wedding dress can take a long time and a lot of effort, as the perfect fit and style are essential - this dress will showcase the bride's loveliness on the day that all eyes will be on her. It is a dress worn just once and then only recalled in memories and photographs thereafter, so it has to be flawless.

Finding and reserving the location of the ceremony and reception can often be a herculean endeavor in and of itself, as the different requirements from the families and the engaged couple need to be considered. There can be hundreds of other details, from tuxedos, to flowers, to chauffeurs, to music, to selecting an officiant - all of these choices require the utmost attention and agreement. It can be a stressful situation, as the couple may have differing opinions from their family, or even from each other. Many of us know of weddings that have gone off the rails during the planning and preparation stage precisely due to these pressures, and therefore the ability to calmly compromise is necessary throughout the process. Trying to pull off the perfect wedding can be so intense that couples often spend their honeymoons simply recovering from the work of putting it all together; after finally catching their breath, they can begin to relax and start their marriage journey in a more blissful state.

Of course, no wedding celebration would be complete without extravagant food, drink, and cake – in fact, such refreshments are often the largest part of the entire wedding budget. Guests are expected to be wined and dined as they offer their congratulations to the happy couple and their families. The fact that eating and drinking have always been such important components of wedding celebrations is reflected in the first public miracle in the ministry of Jesus Christ, which took place at a local wedding that He attended.

"On the third day a wedding took place at Cana in Galilee. Jesus' mother was there, and Jesus and his disciples had also been invited to the wedding. When the wine was gone, Jesus' mother said to him, 'They have no more wine.' 'Woman, why do you involve me?' Jesus replied. 'My hour has not yet come.' His mother said to the servants, 'Do whatever he tells you.' Nearby stood six stone water jars, the kind used by the Jews for ceremonial washing, each holding from twenty to thirty gallons. Jesus said to the servants, 'Fill the jars with water'; so they filled them to the brim. Then he told them, 'Now draw some out and take it to the master of the banquet.' They did so, and the master of the banquet tasted the water that had been turned into wine. He did not realize where it had come from, though the servants who had drawn the water knew. Then he called the bridegroom aside and said, 'Everyone brings out the choice wine first and then the cheaper wine after the guests have had too much to drink; but you have saved the best till now.' What Jesus did here in Cana of Galilee was the first of the signs through which he revealed his glory; and his disciples believed in him" (John 2:1-11, NIV).

Jesus exhibited His power through this miracle, which caused His disciples to gain faith in Him, not just as a rabbi, but as something more. He also took the opportunity to show a huge amount of grace as well. The families of the newlyweds would undoubtedly have been utterly shamed if it became known that they had run out of wine during the middle of the celebration. Such a gaffe would have caused their guests to lose respect for them.

The hosts would have been labelled as being too cheap to procure enough wine, or not fastidious in having the requisite amount of drink prepared. Thankfully, one special guest of theirs was able to gracefully provide a miraculous (and delicious) solution to their shortcoming. We see in this story that the social pressure to have a flawless wedding celebration that is so prevalent in our modern culture was present even in Biblical times.

In today's weddings, on the actual day of

the ceremony, after all the preparations have been made, the long-discussed plans are finally put into motion. The wedding chapel is spotless, and abuzz with activity. Flowers are brought in to add life and color. Candles are lit to set the mood. A long white carpet is laid down the aisle, where the bride and her father will make their slow walk to the front of the chapel. Portraits are positioned, gifts are registered, and music begins to play.

Guests, impeccably dressed and styled, begin to arrive and take their seats. The minister takes his place and prepares to officiate the ceremony. The groomsmen accompany the man of the hour into the chapel - entering single, excited to become a husband. The flower girl and the ring boy, innocent and oblivious, begin to walk down the aisle, followed by the bridesmaids in their matching dresses.

Then finally the moment that all have been waiting for arrives. A hush falls over the crowd as they await to see the beautiful bride, a snapshot of perfection in earthly form. The minister announces her arrival, and in what has now become a ubiquitous wedding ritual in our culture, the officiant asks for all in attendance to please rise from their seats as she enters.

Everyone in the chapel stands, jostling to get a peek, standing on the tips of their toes to get a view of her coming down the aisle. Musical instruments begin playing the familiar melody of "Here Comes the Bride", the doors open, and absolutely every eye in the room is fixed on the bride. She enters in, arm in arm with her father, and walks to the altar where she will transform from young lady to wife, and become one with her husband.

The bride slowly marches down the aisle, surrounded by her friends, family, and guests - all standing quietly in awe of her beauty. The floral bouquet she holds in her hands is a token of life and youth, but the flowers pale in comparison to the blossom that she has become. The bride, dressed in white to symbolize purity, offers her heart and promises her future to the groom in return for his. The couple meet at the front of the chapel, take their position before man and God to declare their love, exchange their vows, and make a covenant commitment to each other, until death do they part.

So how do the rituals and symbolism of a marriage ceremony relate to the call to stand during worship? Just as all of the wedding guests stand as the bride enters, in awe of her beauty, we stand as the Lord enters our place of worship, overwhelmed by the beauty of who He is. In wedding ceremonies, it is the bride who is the center of attention; in our worship, all eyes are fixed upon the Lord, who is the center of the very universe.

His radiance compels us to turn our gaze away from the things of this world, like a bolt of lightning in the midst of a storm, or like the striking of a match in a dark cave, or like bright stars shining out from the night - we cannot help but to look at the light. We are drawn to Him, "fixing our eyes on Jesus, the pioneer and perfecter of faith. For the joy set before him he endured the cross, scorning its shame, and sat down at the right hand of the throne of God" (Hebrews 12:2, NIV).

God shines white in glory not just to symbolize purity, but being purity itself – righteous and holy above all. The Lord is the perfect incarnation of all the ideals that the bride is supposed to represent - the paragon of beauty, purity, grace, commitment, and love. He accepts us as His own, and we now live in the covenent that He has made with His people. We stand as God enters in, to honor who He is, and what He has done for us. The music of heaven echoes through the air, and we break our stunned silence to join with all creation in singing praise to our God.

And as we wait for the day when we can join Him in our heavenly home, we know that He hovers over us, and covers us with His presence like a canopy. He will always be faithful to us, and He will lead us to the true Promised Land, to live with Him forever. The Lord has made a covenant commitment to us, one that can never be broken, for it was sealed not by vows or the exchange of rings, but instead was sealed by the blood of the Lamb.

From the beginning of time, the love story between God and His people has been made clear. He declares over us, "I have loved you with an everlasting love; therefore I have continued my faithfulness to you" (Jeremiah 31:3, ESV). The institution of marriage itself was designed by God to teach us about what our relationship with our Creator is like, and to be a metaphor for it - an object lesson and a physical representation of the covenant between the Lord and His people.

The Bible refers to the Church as the bride of Christ, betrothed to our blessed Savior, and the Word teaches married couples how they are to love by using the example of God's sacrifice and service to His chosen people. "Wives, submit to your own husbands, as to the Lord. For the husband is the head of the wife even as Christ is the head of the church, his body, and is himself its Savior. Now as the church submits to Christ, so also wives should submit in everything to their husbands. Husbands, love your wives, as Christ loved the church and gave himself up for her, that he might sanctify her, having cleansed her by the washing of water with the word, so that he might present the church to himself in splendor, without spot or wrinkle or any such thing, that she might be holy and without blemish" (Ephesians 5:22-27, ESV). What good news it is for us, that Jesus has removed all of our imperfections, and now we are spotless and clean before His eyes.

And what good news it is for His beloved bride, the church, that all of the planning and hard work that goes into getting ready for an earthly wedding will utterly pale in comparison with the preparation that God is doing for our arrival into our heavenly home. Jesus said, "Believe in God; believe also in me. In my Father's house are many rooms. If it were not so, would I have told you that I go to prepare a place for you? And if I go and prepare a place for you, I will come again and will take you to myself, that where I am you may be also" (John 14:1-3, ESV). Jesus is preparing paradise for us; He will not forget or forsake us, and one day we will join Him there.

In Biblical Israel, when a man proposed to his intended and she accepted, the young man would work for the entire year-long engagement period to prepare a place for them to live after the wedding. He would go to his father's house and build a new dwelling for him and his new wife to begin their lives together. What an amazing metaphor that Jesus used when teaching His people that He is preparing a place for us in Heaven.

And if all the grandeur and perfection of an earthly wedding celebration can be accomplished after only a few months of work, how much grander and more perfect will it be when we finally enter our heavenly home, which Jesus has been preparing for us this whole time? We long for this paradise and the shalom (peace) to come, which the Bible describes as such: "And I saw the holy city, new Jerusalem, coming down out of heaven from God, prepared as a bride adorned for her husband. And I heard a loud voice from the throne saying, "Behold, the dwelling place of God is with man. He will dwell with them, and they will be his people, and God himself will be with them as their God. He will wipe away every tear from their eyes, and death shall be no more, neither shall there be mourning, nor crying, nor pain anymore, for the former things have passed away" (Revelations 21:2-4, ESV). Amen! Come Lord Jesus!

Marriage is such a beautiful analogy for our relationship with God, and the ritual of standing for the bride's entrance reminds us that He is worthy of all honor and praise. As the Lord enters, let us stand in awe of His beauty and grace. Let us rise and fix our eyes on Him alone. Let us stand strong, trusting in the promise that He has made, to keep His covenant with us, knowing that He will be faithful to us in all ways. Let us stand and worship our God.

One thing I ask from the Lord, this only do I seek:
that I may dwell in the house of the Lord
all the days of my life,
to gaze on the beauty of the Lord
and to seek him in his temple.
(Psalms 27:4, NIV)

HANDS
LIFTED UP

Let us lift up our hearts
and our hands
to God in heaven
(Lamentations 3:41, NIV)

Jehovah Jireh - God is our provider, but in our vanity and self-reliance, it is often only at the end of our own devices that we turn to Him as a last resort. This is a theme found throughout the Bible, as many of the characters within the Scriptures find themselves in just that kind of situation, a prime example being the life of King David. He is described in the Bible as being a man after God's own heart, but has a personal history that can best be described as a rollercoaster ride - filled with twists and turns that send him on emotional highs, followed by episodes where his life seems to be crashing down. But through it all, his trust in the steadfast love of God remains, and David endeavors not to lose hope but instead to live out a life of faith, whether in green pastures or in the valley of the shadow of death.

This faith is evident in his writing, as he was one of the authors of the Book of Psalms. Through these written works, David encourages us to lift our hands in worship and prayer, in times of both celebration and lamentation. Whether by quiet waters or in dry desert places, he reminds us that it does not matter what our current situation may be; regardless of everything, God is still worthy of praise - worthy of worship with hands raised. As David writes, "You, God, are my God, earnestly I seek you; I thirst for you, my whole being longs for you, in a dry and parched land where there is no water. I have seen you in the sanctuary and beheld your power and your glory. Because your love is better than life, my lips will glorify you. I will praise you as long as I live, and in your name I will lift up my hands" (Psalms 63:1-4, ESV).

Victory

But thanks be to God,
who gives us the victory
through our Lord Jesus Christ.
(1 Corinthians 15:57, ESV)

Go to any sporting event and examine the crowd. See what they do when their team scores. Think about what happens on any touchdown in a game of football - the referee races down the goal line with both hands extended above his head.

Think of the gymnast who has stuck the perfect landing. Think of the sprinter as they break the finish line first. Raised hands are used throughout the world of sports as a sign of victory. As we worship, we raise our hands to declare that God has won the ultimate victory - He is our eternal champion.

The people of Israel were intimately familiar with the kind of victory that was possible when God was on their side. There is a battle described in the Book of Exodus, chapter 17, where in the middle of their journey to the Promised Land, the Israelites were attacked by another nation, the Amalekites. Moses, the leader of Israel, ordered his second-in-command Joshua to lead the fighting men into battle, and then proceeded up a hill to watch over the conflict with two companions. As he watched the battle rage on below, Moses raised his hands above the battleground, and the Israelites were able to push back their enemy.

However, Moses started to become tired as the fighting continued, and began to lower his hands. When that happened, the tide of the battle turned for the Amalekites. So his companions helped him raise his hands up again, and the Israelite army regained the upper hand, and ultimately defeated their enemy. Moses built an altar for the nation to remember what had happened there, and named the altar, "The Lord is my Banner", referring to the unique nature of the battle. Moses reminded the people that it was not by their own might, but because hands were raised to God, as if placed upon the throne of the Lord, that they were able to secure the victory.

What exactly was going on in this battle? Did the ultimate outcome depend on the men who were fighting, or did it depend on whether Moses was raising or lowering his hands? Did it therefore depend not upon warriors or their weapons, but ultimately on God himself? And if that was the case, and God was solely responsible for the victory, then for what reason did the men of Israel even have to take up arms?

It had been previously demonstrated to them that God could wipe out whole armies without human help. That was obviously the case when the forces of Egypt were destroyed as the Red Sea collapsed upon them while they were chasing the Israelites. "That day the Lord saved Israel from the hands of the Egyptians, and Israel saw the Egyptians lying dead on the shore. And when the Israelites saw the mighty hand of the Lord displayed against the Egyptians, the people feared the Lord and put their trust in him and in Moses his servant" (Exodus 14:30-31, NIV). Having been newly released from slavery and bondage, God destroyed the Egyptians to show the Hebrews that He would protect them and fight for them, now that they were free.

Against the Amalekites, it is clear that God was teaching the nation of Israel a slightly different lesson - one in which they were involved, yet still reliant upon the Lord. Even though they were the ones on the battleground doing the fighting, the actual victory ultimately came from God Himself. And by the course of the battle changing every time Moses raised or lowered his hands, it taught them, as it teaches us today, that it is only by holding on to Him alone that we can be successful in our own battles. The Bible encourages us, "Be strong and courageous. Do not be afraid; do not be discouraged, for the Lord your God will be with you wherever you go" (Joshua 1:9, NIV).

Let us lift up our hands to the throne of the Lord as we worship. Let us lift up all of our struggles to God, knowing that He is our Banner as well – and that every battle belongs to the Lord. Take courage, knowing that "The Lord will fight for you; you need only to be still" (Exodus 14:14, NIV). Let us lift up our hands to worship our King, the source of all our hope and ultimate victory.

Come Out with Your Hands Up

Humble yourselves before the Lord,
and he will exalt you.
(James 4:10, ESV)

At the end of every fight, every battle, and every war, there is a winner and a loser - those who are victorious and those who are defeated. And in every defeat, there is a moment when those who have lost know that their situation is hopeless, and are therefore at the mercy of their enemy. What a terrifying moment that must be, to become fully aware of your helplessness, and to be completely vanquished. At that point, a decision must be made on whether to continue the forlorn fight, or to embrace surrender and ask for mercy.

When the time comes to lay down their arms and acknowledge their situation, the feeling of dread and fear among the losing side must be overwhelming, as it permeates throughout their hearts and bodies. Uncertain if their lives will continue past the next moment, those who have committed to surrender know that they have no other choice than to raise the white flag, and move out into the open - fully exposed and vulnerable to their adversaries. To prove their intent, the defeated raise their hands to show that they are weaponless and unable to fight any longer. It is a universally recognized posture that has been used throughout history to display submission and surrender.

The very act of surrendering can literally take the fight out of you, an example of which can be found in the famous speech given by Chief Joseph of the Nez Perce. In 1877, a short war was fought between the US Army and members of the Nez Perce nation, which lasted only a few months. This war started when several tribes in the Pacific Northwest refused to renounce their claims to their ancestral lands to the American government and settlers, as a result of the poor treatment that these people had received from the United States. Even members of the U.S. Army charged with fighting these native forces had opinions contrary to their assigned task, as American General Philip H. Sheridan commented, "We took away their country and their means of support, broke up their mode of living, their habits of life, introduced disease and decay among them and it was for this and against this they made war. Could anyone expect less?"[i]

The Nez Perce warriors were vastly out-numbered and outgunned, but still bravely fought a series of battles and skirmishes as they tried to make their way to safety in Canada, a journey that would take them over a thousand miles. However, their struggle would ultimately end in defeat just 40 miles from the border, at the Battle of Bear Paw. During the capitulation ceremony, held on October 5th, 1877, Chief Joseph of the Nez Perce surrendered to the U.S. Army, and his speech was recorded by those in attendance. "I am tired of fighting. Our chiefs are killed. Looking Glass is dead. Toohoolhoolzoote is dead. The old men are all dead. It is the young men who say, "Yes" or "No". He who led the young men is dead. It is cold, and we have no blankets. The little children are freezing to death. My people, some of them, have run away to the hills, and have no blankets, no food. No one knows where they are -- perhaps freezing to death. I want to have time to look for my children and see how many of them I can find. Maybe I shall find them among the dead. Hear me, my chiefs! I am tired. My heart is sick and sad. From where the sun now stands I will fight no more forever."[ii] You can feel in these words that Chief Joseph's will to resist is completely gone, and he has embraced defeat to the point where he pledges never to take up arms again.

Soldiers surrender by raising empty hands to the opposing army, criminals surrender by raising empty hands to law enforcement – this act displays for all to see that they have given up. They must come out into the open without weapons, completely vulnerable and utterly exposed - and this is exactly what we are called to emulate in worship before our God. Our pride and sinful nature have no defense before His righteousness. There is no weapon that we could use to attack God's holiness when we are exposed before Him. There is no justification for our iniquities when our hearts are fully revealed in the light of His glory.

There is nothing we can hide from an all-knowing God, as King David wrote, "You have searched me, Lord, and you know me. You know when I sit and when I rise; you perceive my thoughts from afar. You discern my going out and my lying down; you are familiar with all my ways. Before a word is on my tongue you, Lord, know it completely. You hem me in behind and before, and you lay your hand upon me. Such knowledge is too wonderful for me, too lofty for me to attain. Where can I go from your Spirit? Where can I flee from your presence? If I go up to the heavens, you are there; if I make my bed in the depths, you are there. If I rise on the wings of the dawn, if I settle on the far side of the sea, even there your hand will guide me, your right hand will hold me fast. If I say, 'Surely the darkness will hide me and the light become night around me,' even the darkness will not be dark to you; the night will shine like the day, for darkness is as light to you" (Psalms 139:1-12, NIV). It is absolute foolishness to think that we can come before God without every secret and hidden thought or action being uncovered – He will bring our sinful nature out into the open and into the light.

That which is secret to man is revealed to God. That which is hidden in man's heart is plain to see for the Lord. Just as a watchmaker can open up a timepiece to see all of the moving parts inside, our Creator looks at us in the same way. The Bible gives another example, explaining that, "We are the clay, you are the potter; we are all the work of your hand" (Isaiah 64:8, NIV). So what point is there in pretending to be anything else other than who we truly are in front of the One who formed us. No fight can be mustered in the presence of His glory - the only response we could possibly have is to surrender with our hands raised, as we cry out for mercy.

Sometimes in the process of surrender, the defeated party looks to negotiate a quicker end to hostilities in return for keeping some privileges. But when we come before God Almighty, there can be no negotiation - there is no leverage that we can hold against the Maker of Heaven and Earth. When man submits to God, it is always an unconditional sur-render, or it is no surrender at all. We cannot parley better terms to Him - instead we must come before the Lord on His terms alone, with empty and outstretched hands.

Looking at the etymology of the word surrender, we can glean even more about approaching God with this attitude. It comes from the Old French word 'Surrendre' and the root of the word means 'render over', 'deliver over', or 'to give up'. The word picture is that of a defeated country having to give up control of territory to their foes, like what the Nez Perce were forced to do at the end of their war. How fitting it is that we are called to surrender to God in all things - we give up control and deliver over our lives, our future, our everything to Him.

Jesus demands this absolute commitment from us, as He said, "those of you who do not give up everything you have cannot be my disciples" (Luke 14:33, NIV). We must submit completely to His authority, though we recognize that ceding control over our lives to God can be an intimidating proposition. But instead of fearing this total surrender, we should embrace it, because through it we exchange that which is temporal for that which is eternal. As Jesus said, "For whoever wants to save their life will lose it, but whoever loses their life for me will find it. What good will it be for someone to gain the whole world, yet forfeit their soul? Or what can anyone give in exchange for their soul?" (Matthew 16:25-26, NIV).

The end result of our surrender is not imprisonment or destruction, but instead it is acceptance and healing. We render over control, and we receive true peace, the kind of peace that surpasses all understanding. As Jesus said, "Peace I leave with you; my peace I give to you. Not as the world gives do I give to you. Let not your hearts be troubled, neither let them be afraid" (John 14:27, ESV). And as we continue to grow in faith, our transformation continues towards becoming completely like our Jesus. As the Apostle Paul wrote, "I have been crucified with Christ and I no longer live, but Christ lives in me. The life I now live in the body, I live by faith in the Son of God, who loved me and gave himself for me" (Galatians 2:20, NIV).

The Bible offers many examples of what total surrender looks like. There is the story of Abraham's unimaginable commitment to God in the Book of Genesis, where he was willing to go so far as sacrificing his own son Isaac when the Lord tested him to do so. Abraham displayed great faith, going to the point of picking up a knife to perform the sacrifice, reasoning that even if Isaac died, God could bring him back to life. But at the last moment, God stops Abraham and provides a substitute to take Isaac's place on the altar.

The story of the Cross closely mirrors the story of Abraham and Isaac, where another beloved son is taken to be sacrificed - but in this case, it was God's own Son. We see the total surrender of Jesus to the Father's plan as He prepared for His greatest work upon the Cross. Christ struggled with what He had to do, but in the end declared, "not my will, but yours be done" (Luke 22:42, NIV). That is full surrender, the ultimate example of laying down everything before God and His will.

So, in response to who God is and what He has done for us, let us worship with hands raised, in total surrender before our victorious Lord. There is no pretense to be had at the foot of the Cross; we know that anything we try to hide behind is rendered useless by the One who sees to the very core of us. We give up our old lives, who we once were, and embrace what we are called to become - as the Bible tells us, "Therefore, if anyone is in Christ, the new creation has come: The old has gone, the new is here!" (2 Corinthians 5:17, NIV).

As we are lovingly overcome let us give all that we have to God, knowing that in reality, what we get from capitulating is better than anything we could try to hold on to. As Jesus said, "The kingdom of heaven is like treasure hidden in a field. When a man found it, he hid it again, and then in his joy went and sold all he had and bought that field" (Matthew 13:44, NIV). We joyfully embrace defeat so that we can gain the greatest victory. Let us therefore raise our hands in worship, empty and defenseless, fully surrendered before the Lord.

Little Children

Jesus said,
"Let the little children come to me,
and do not hinder them,
for the kingdom of heaven
belongs to such as these."

(Matthew 19:14, NIV)

"Behold, children are a gift of the Lord, the fruit of the womb is a reward" (Psalms 127:3, NASB). Little children are blessedly innocent, free from the cynicism and negativity found so often in adults - they take life as one happy day after another. We can learn so much from them about what it means to love unconditionally, and how to live with a child-like faith.

Jesus even used the example of children to teach His disciples about their hearts and how they should live. "At that time the disciples came to Jesus, saying, 'Who is the greatest in the kingdom of heaven?' And calling to him a child, he put him in the midst of them and said, 'Truly, I say to you, unless you turn and become like children, you will never enter the kingdom of heaven. Whoever humbles himself like this child is the greatest in the kingdom of heaven'" (Matthew 18:1-4, ESV).

Christians are often exhorted to seek after childlike faith, but what exactly sets that kind of faith apart from other ways that adults believe? Children believe in the impossible, just from hearing it from their mother or father. It is the kind of faith that does not need to see in order to believe, and it comes from being the recipient of much love.

This is what the Bible tells us about love: "It always protects, always trusts, always hopes, always perseveres. Love never fails" (1 Corinthians 13:7-8, NIV). Because of the great love that they have received from their parents, children are able to put their complete trust in everything they hear from them, even the fantastical.

Children believe in stories, in fairy tales, and in make-believe - this kind of imaginative play is essential to their mental development. However, as people grow, so does our bitterness - every injury, whether physical, emotional, or spiritual, reinforces our perceived need to shield ourselves against the next possible source of pain. And in doing so, our hearts begin to close off from the beauty and wonder that still exists in the world, and makes it so much harder for us to put trust in others.

Older children will tease younger ones for still believing in fantasies. Sadly, as we age, we start to lose our childlike faith as we come face-to-face with the hard realities of our world. But the truth is that we actually need more wonder in our lives, not less, and children remind us of that. The world already has enough malice and despair in it, as well as being full of the mundane and unremarkable; therefore, having the ability to believe should not be belittled, but rather encouraged.

Sometimes a child's imagination can take a turn for the worse, leading to nightmares that cause them to run to their parents' bedside. Children know that in the arms of their father or mother, they are safe and secure. Or consider toddlers who are learning how to walk, and the joy they find once they start exploring the world on their own. But at any moment, they know that without even saying a word, they can raise their hands in a universal sign that instantly communicates their desire to be held and lifted up.

This action can also happen in a moment of discipline, in which the child has done something wrong and is being reprimanded for it. After the father or mother has expressed their disappointment and frustration with their child, there is a need to reassure them physically. Though the child might have behaved poorly, even at those moments they can still raise their little arms, and through their parent's embrace they are reminded that they are still loved and cherished.

From the moment a baby is born, they are completely dependent on their mother and father to provide for their every need. Babies are born with a tremendous ability to grip, their tiny fists filled with more strength than one would assume. They use this power from the beginning of their lives to physically hold on to those who love them the most. Little children cling to their parents, and even as they grow and mature, they continue to find shelter in their guardians' arms.

As soon as they feel a hint of danger or uncertainty, children can race back to mom and dad, knowing that nothing can harm them under the shadow of their parents' wings. They can hold their arms up, and within a fraction of a second, the parent will instinctively respond by picking them up in their arms. When children get hurt, when they get sad, or when they fear, they know they can run to their father's arms and find safety and security.

In worship, don't we share this same instinct, to turn to our Heavenly Father, and raise our hands to have Him hold us close? We will face many dangers, toils, and snares in this life, but through it all, "God is our refuge and strength, an ever-present help in trouble. Therefore we will not fear, though the earth give way and the mountains fall into the heart of the sea, though its waters roar and foam and the mountains quake with their surging" (Psalms 46:1-2, NIV). The Lord will be with us in every situation.

Our Good Father will defend us, and will protect us through every hardship we face. What blessed assurance is ours, as we hear God's voice saying to us, "Fear not, for I have redeemed you; I have called you by name, you are mine. When you pass through the waters, I will be with you; and through the rivers, they shall not overwhelm you; when you walk through fire you shall not be burned, and the flame shall not consume you. For I am the Lord your God, the Holy One of Israel, your Savior" (Isaiah 43:1-3, ESV). He has called us by name, He has claimed us each as His own, and there is nothing that can take us away from Him.

When we are hurt, when we are lonely, we can run to the Father for safety and security, for no one and nothing can break the bond that God has with us. To His children, the Lord declares, "I give them eternal life, and they will never perish, and no one will snatch them out of my hand" (John 10:28,

ESV). What a relief it is, that our Heavenly Father will not turn away from us, but just like an earthly father He holds us in His arms, and provides the comfort and shelter we need. We rejoice in our adoption into His family, as the Bible says, "See what great love the Father has lavished on us, that we should be called children of God! And that is what we are!" (1 John 3:1, NIV).

Parents understand that sometimes discipline is required when raising children, but these corrective actions come only out of their love for their child, not out of anger or hate. The Word of God teaches, "Whoever spares the rod hates their children, but the one who loves their children is careful to discipline them" (Proverbs 13:24, NIV). Parents want the very best for their children, and so redirect them from what is harmful to what is good for them through discipline.

God does the same with His children, always leading us away from what is harmful to what is good. Therefore, when we go through a period of receiving reprimand or rebuke, we should not be discouraged. "No discipline seems pleasant at the time, but painful. Later on, however, it produces a harvest of righteousness and peace for those who have been trained by it" (Hebrews 12:11, NIV). Disciplinary actions lead to spiritual growth, and are actually reminders of His love for us. If God did not love us, then why would He spend any time or effort in trying to teach us the right path? As the Lord says, "Those whom I love I rebuke and discipline. So be earnest and repent" (Revelation 3:19, NIV).

Just as no loving parent would ever refuse their child when they lift their hands to be held, our Heavenly Father will not refuse us as well. He says to us, "So do not fear, for I am with you; do not be dismayed, for I am your God. I will strengthen you and help you; I will uphold you with my righteous right hand" (Isaiah 41:10, NIV). Even in the hardest moments of raising children, instinct drives parents to have an immediate physical reaction when they see their child holding up their arms – that instinct was placed there by our Creator, as we were made in His image. It doesn't matter if the child is misbehaving, if they are in the midst of a frustrating tantrum, or if they are causing an embarrassing scene - when the child comes to the father with arms outstretched, the father will respond with love and acceptance, not rejection.

How wonderful it is to worship like little children, lifting our arms to our Father, seeking His embrace. We echo the cry of the Psalmist: "Be merciful to me, O God, be merciful to me, for in you my soul takes refuge; in the shadow of your wings I will take refuge, till the storms of destruction pass by" (Psalms 57:1, ESV). In our times of worship, let us be like children, safe in the loving arms of our Good Father. He will not refuse us. He will bend low, pick us up, and will hold us close to His heart, as He whispers reminders of His great love for us. We are His children, so let us approach Him confidently, with arms raised, knowing that we will be embraced. Let us worship with hands lifted high.

> *O Lord, I call upon you; hasten to me!*
> *Give ear to my voice when I call to you!*
> *Let my prayer be counted as incense before you,*
> *and the lifting up of my hands*
> *as the evening sacrifice!*
> *(Psalms 141:1-2, ESV)*

BOW DOWN

As I live, says the Lord,
every knee shall bow to me,
and every tongue shall confess to God.
(Romans 14:11, ESV)

Bowing can take many forms - the slightest nod of the head could be considered a bow. Common in Asian cultures is the reverent bow of greeting, often used to display deference to elders. In the Christian faith, believers will at times get on their knees in prayer, to show their deep commitment as they lay their requests at the feet of God. There is also the ancient practice of prostration, where supplicants will lay their bodies flat on the floor as the ultimate demonstration of humility in worship.

Though acts of bowing and kneeling exist in many different forms, they all have one thing in common: they display respect and veneration to the one being bowed before. God is worthy of such worship, for who He is, and for what He has done. As the Psalmist writes, "I will bow down toward your holy temple and will praise your name for your unfailing love and your faithfulness" (Psalms 138:2, NIV).

Such worship is pleasing to God, as it physically displays a humbled spirit before Him, and He rewards those who approach with such an attitude. The Bible says, "Though the Lord is exalted, he looks kindly on the lowly; though lofty, he sees them from afar" (Psalms 138:6, NIV). We are called to bow in worship, to show our utmost reverence before the Lord. Here are several pictures that capture the posture of our hearts as we praise our Holy God on our knees.

A Beggar's Posture

But she came and knelt before him,
saying, "Lord, help me."
(Matthew 15:25, ESV)

Life is full of hardship, as even our Savior warned us, "In this world you will have trouble" (John 16:33, NIV). In truth, we are all one wrong turn away from losing everything we hold dear. The Bible reminds us of our frail condition, saying, "What is your life? For you are a mist that appears for a little time and then vanishes" (James 4:14, ESV). Our very existence is extremely fragile, but the fallacious nature of this world deceives us into thinking that we can somehow create our own security, and that we can maintain the lives we want by our own power or effort. We shield ourselves behind our health, status, career, relationships, wealth, and a myriad of other devices. That is foolishness of the highest degree, as none of these things last, they all will deteriorate in the end. How many examples can we find throughout history where the strong have become weak, the rich have become poor, and the wise have become fools.

If we can honestly recognize the delicate nature of our mortal existence, then we cannot escape the fact that life is in many ways like hanging over a cliff by a rope. Part of our rat race mentality is to foolishly compare ourselves with others hanging onto their own ropes, and judging how much more perilously positioned our neighbors are. But even the luckiest, most fortunate, and most blessed people will, at one point or other (and often many more times than just once), find themselves close to falling off the cliff, without the resources or wisdom to overcome the problems in their lives.

So, what do we do when we find ourselves precariously poised over the precipice? What do we do when all of our clever solutions are gone, and when we have no options left in front of us? The answer is simple - we beg. We cast down the false crowns of independence and self-reliance, throw ourselves to the ground, and implore anyone willing to listen for help.

The posture of begging is simple, unsophisticated, and primal. It is to get on our knees, as a sign that we are powerless, and show that we are not worthy to even stand. It is intrinsically humiliating, to place the person we are kneeling before above us, physically and symbolically, and place ourselves below them. All pride, strength, and self-confidence are gone - begging is desperation in physical form.

Examples of this posture can be found throughout the Gospels, in stories of both the rich and poor, and the mighty and the pitiful. These narratives are about people who have realized that they are powerless to solve their problems without God's help, so they search Jesus out and plead before Him on their knees. A prime example can be found in the Book of Mark, which describes the scene as such: "When Jesus had again crossed over by boat to the other side of the lake, a large crowd gathered around him while he was by the lake. Then one of the synagogue leaders, named Jairus, came, and when he saw Jesus, he fell at his feet. He pleaded earnestly with him, 'My little daughter is dying. Please come and put your hands on her so that she will be healed and live.' So Jesus went with him" (Mark 5:21-24, NIV).

The description of Jairus in the Scriptures is sparse – we learn that he is a synagogue leader, and that role in that culture would have made him an important and respected person in the community. The other truth we can derive about him is that he has a daughter who he obviously loves deeply. We do not know how much he knew about Jesus, or if he understood who Jesus truly was, but it is clear that Jairus had heard enough to know that there was something special about this man from Nazareth. We know that conflict occurs later between Jesus and the ruling elite, but where Jairus falls into that context has been lost to history.

Jairus may have been a powerful man, but because of his daughter's life-threatening condition, he had exhausted the limits of his own power, and is put in the situation where he had to try anything to save her. Doubtless, this loving father must have prayed fervently to God for healing. And we can be sure that he had done all within his means to help his little girl, scratching one idea after another until he had no other options, with both time and hope quickly running out. Fortunately for Jairus, a new rabbi who had been building up a reputation as a miracle worker was within traveling distance, and so he seized the opportunity to beseech this Jesus of Nazareth.

Certainly, respected synagogue leaders did not easily beg on their knees in public, but what else could Jairus do? Jesus was his last hope, and therefore Jairus had no other choice but to try to convince this Healer to help his daughter. He fell at the feet of the Messiah, kneeling as he finally let go of his own power and showed true faith - the faith of a father with a sick child. This faith that Jairus displayed immediately bore fruit, as the Bible tells us that Jesus went with him to heal his daughter.

What a deep and desperate faith it is, to be the parent of a sick child. To go through something that you would not wish upon your worst enemy, and to be shaken to the very core, out of fear for your child's life and well-being. That is how powerful the love between parent and child is. Despite what the worldly media would have our culture believe, it is not romantic love that is the most important and purest love of all, but rather it is the love between parent and child that is paramount. This is one of the reasons why God the Father and Jesus Christ are described as being Father and Son, so that we humans could comprehend just a tiny fraction of what that relationship must be like. And how deep the Father's love for us must be, that He willingly sacrificed His own Son so that we might live.

What parent would not give every earthly possession they had to buy health for their child? Is there a price you could place on something like that? What expense would Jairus not have spared in search of a cure for his beloved daughter? He humbled himself on his knees in front of Jesus, in full view of the crowd gathered there – in an honor-based culture, what could have been more valuable to a man of respect than his own personal reputation? Jairus found himself with nothing left to lose, and only his faith to hold on to - and by the grace of God, he found the one person in the world who actually had the power to heal his sick child.

Coming to the house, Jairus is informed that his daughter had died, but "Jesus told him, 'Don't be afraid; just believe'" (Mark 5:36, NIV). The reaction of Jairus to the news of her death is not recorded in the Gospels, but his faith must have been the only reason he did not fall apart at that moment. Jesus took the parents to the child's body in private, away from the crowds, then "He took her by the hand and said to her, 'Talitha koum!' (which means 'Little girl, I say to you, get up!'). Immediately the girl stood up and began to walk around (she was twelve years old). At this they were completely astonished" (Mark 5:41-42, NIV). Jairus was rewarded for his faith, and though he is not mentioned further in the narrative, without a doubt this miracle must have left him a changed man.

The kind of faith that Jairus displayed was not limited to just the respected members of that society. Consider the leper described in the first chapter of the Book of Mark, who by all outward appearances was the polar opposite of Jairus. This story recounts another miracle by Jesus, but in this case the supplicant's name was not important enough to be included, as this man had nothing but his illness to define him. He was deemed as a nobody, but somehow remains as a model of faith for us to recognize and learn from, even to this day.

To be leprous in Jewish society at that time was to be cast out from everything you had ever known. Leprosy was feared for being highly contagious, and was interpreted by that culture as being a physical manifestation of the punishment for sin. The people of Israel were instructed to maintain ritual cleanliness, as God told them, "I am the Lord your God; consecrate yourselves and be holy, because I am holy" (Leviticus 11:44, NIV). Lepers were expelled from their communities in part to maintain that cleanliness, and actually had to announce to anyone approaching them that they were unclean. In that culture, if the goal in life was to be set apart for righteousness, then to be infected with this terrible disease was almost the complete antithesis of that goal. It was as if lepers were set apart in the wrong direction, unacceptable for any part in society but to be avoided and shunned.

Exiled from their family and from their community, lepers were sent away to live alone, or in groups with others who were also diseased. No effective medicine or treatment existed for the condition at the time, but would that have stopped someone who was infected from pursuing all possible remedies? If we somehow found ourselves in the same position, wouldn't we have used up all of our resources to chase after cures, or to seek out doctors or shamans, to try to find healing?

Lepers were told to stay away from people, as a safeguard against infecting others. So imagine the desperation of this anonymous sick man, to break that cardinal rule and come begging before Jesus, as described in the Book of Mark. With no alternative, and with nothing left to lose, he recklessly came close to others when no one wanted him near, and he spoke when no one wanted to hear him.

It was a desperate faith that compelled this leper to seek Jesus out and fall at His feet. "A man with leprosy came to him and begged him on his knees, 'If you are willing, you can make me clean'" (Mark 1:40, NIV). The reaction from Jesus must have been utterly shocking to witnesses, as it was the exact opposite of what they would have expected a reasonable person to do. "Moved with compassion, Jesus reached out with His hand and touched him, and said to him, 'I am willing; be cleansed.' And immediately the leprosy left him, and he was cleansed" (Mark 1:41-42, NASB).

This simple touch was an exemplar of grace - obviously, Jesus would have been able to heal this man from a distance, as He had displayed that ability in other public miracles. But instead, He deliberately chose to place His hand upon the sick man, breaking all kinds of health codes, rabbinical teaching, and general common sense. It was understood at the time that leprosy could spread by touch, but by reaching out, Jesus showed that healing could spread by touch as well. Fear of this terrible disease was great, but by placing His hand on the infected man, Christ showed His power to be greater.

It was unimaginable for the people of the time to see a rabbi physically touch a leper, but seeing God do that which is unimaginable is not something that should surprise us. As the Lord declares, "For my thoughts are not your thoughts, neither are your ways my ways" (Isaiah 55:8, NIV). Mere mortals are not capable of fully comprehending the divine, which is evident in the fact that many of the teachings and actions of Jesus were difficult for the original audience to wrap their minds around, this miracle being just one small example. And though modern society might consider itself so much more sophisticated now, the truth is that all of our advances have not changed the fact that our learning

and knowledge remain finite and rudimentary rela-
tive to the glory and greatness of God.

Human wisdom pales in comparison to Biblical truth, as it is written, "God chose the foolish
things of the world to shame the wise" (1 Corinthians 1:27, NIV). Foolish and reckless though this act
of healing by Jesus must have seemed to those who
witnessed it, to the leper it was the perfect ending
to his ordeal. The touch was a gentle reminder that
he was still worthy to God; it was exactly what the
man needed to be fully healed. After years of suffering and exile, it was an act of redemption and restor-
ation of his body - and of his heart.

Having no other options, both Jairus and the
leper begged on their knees before Jesus. Both men
were given grace, mercy, and love - and by the power
of God, healing was poured out for them. What
beautiful symmetry we find at the conclusion of
both accounts: for Jairus and his little girl, the story
begins with the father falling to the ground, and fin-
ishes with the Savior telling the daughter to rise. In
the story of the leper, who broke society's rules by
drawing near to Jesus, Jesus responded by breaking
those same rules with His healing touch.

After being defined for so many years by this
terrible disease, the now-healed (but still unidenti-
fied) man became redefined as a carrier of the Gospel
message. He started to infect others with the love of
God by sharing his testimony of what the Messiah
did for him. The Bible tells us that "he went out and
began to proclaim it freely and to spread the news

around, to such an extent that Jesus could no longer publicly enter a city" (Mark 1:45, NASB). He became a super-spreader of the good news, having been saved from his terminal condition.

Both Jairus and the leper were running out of time, and so without hesitation they just jumped into imploring Jesus. With an urgent boldness born out of their desperate situations, they simply fell at the feet of the Messiah and begged for healing. Seeing the response that Jesus gives them opens the door for us to do the same - to fall before the same Messiah and forgo any of the salutations that typically accompany our prayer and supplication. We are free to follow their example and simply cry out to the Lord in desperation.

Physically, we may or may not currently be in similar circumstances as either Jairus or the leper, but in a spiritual sense we are all equally desperate. We all hunger for the healing of our souls, and long for the Holy Spirit to touch us, just as Jesus touched the leper. Let us throw off the worldly veil of self-reliance that has covered our eyes, and see our fragile condition for what it really is. Let us look past the fallacies of our own power and ability. The truth is that we need God even more than we know.

So let us kneel in desperate faith before the God who is able and willing to heal and restore. Regardless of our resources, status, health, or other circumstances, we are all just one random tragedy away from having our whole world crash down around us. Though we will face many hardships in this world, Jesus comforts us, saying, "But take heart! I have overcome the world" (John 16:33, NIV). The Lord is mighty to save, and we can trust in Him. God invites us to Himself, right from where we are.

He will not turn away from us when we cry out to Him, for "The Lord is near to the broken-hearted and saves the crushed in spirit" (Psalms 34:18, ESV). Let us kneel in worship to our Savior, and beg for His redeeming touch. We long to hear a response like the one the Messiah gave to the Canaanite woman who beseeched Him for healing on her knees: "Then Jesus said to her, 'Woman, you have great faith! Your request is granted'" (Matthew 15:28, NIV). Let us fall down before our God in worship.

Kneel a Man, Rise a Knight

For the Lord your God
is the one who goes with you
to fight for you against your enemies
to give you victory.
(Deuteronomy 20:4, NIV)

There is a well-known European tradition that began hundreds of years ago, and revolves around a ceremony called an accolade. Though that name may seem unfamiliar, the imagery surrounding it is instantly recognizable. It is the ceremonial rite of passage held to celebrate when a man is found worthy of being named a knight, and is dubbed into knighthood by a king. Though it could take many different forms, the classic image of this ceremony involved having the prospective knight on his knees, and being tapped on the shoulders with a sword by the monarch.

Sometimes the accolade was planned and prepared for in advance, and at other times it was held at a moment's notice, as a reward for bravery on the battlefield, or for an extraordinarily loyal act of service. Historically, becoming a knight was a transformational process, in many cases involving someone who was born as a commoner, perhaps just a lowly squire or foot soldier, and then is changed into someone of worth. They enter into the ranks of nobility, and are invited thereafter to sit at the table of kings.

The status of knighthood was bestowed not merely for the sake of the one being knighted, but it was a commissioning, used to designate this person as someone who will serve and protect the kingdom and his lord. This theme of faithful service is deeply linked to the position, which we can see from the etymology of the title itself. The word 'Knight' comes from the Old English word 'Cniht', which meant servant, originally derived from the German word 'Knecht' (meaning 'servant' or 'bondsman').

Interestingly, in Japanese culture, although coming from the other side of the world, the word 'Samurai' also has its etymological roots in the idea of being a servant, or serving a lord. These titles designated them to be more than just warriors to fight in battles, but to be set apart from others to honor and faithfully serve their master. What an illustration for us of what it means to become a servant of God, the King of Kings - to kneel before His majesty, transformed as we receive an eternal calling to serve faithfully, protect the innocent, live justly, and uphold His will - all while having a place by His side.

Knights were expected to behave according to strict guidelines, and to be chivalric in all actions. The Ordene de Chevalerie[iii] is an epic poem, written in the Old French language around the year 1220 A.D., that captured many of the ideals of chivalry. It is a fictional story set in the Kingdom of Jerusalem around the time of the Third Crusade, and tells of how that realm came into conflict with nearby Muslim forces.

The hero of the poem is a knight, Prince Hugh II of Tiberias, who is captured after a battle by Saladin, who was the Sultan of Egypt. The Sultan holds the knight as his prisoner, and during the captivity Saladin learns from Hugh, through his conduct and speech, what it meant to be a Christian knight and live according to the rules of chivalry. Saladin is so impressed by what he learns, that by the end of the story, Saladin desires himself to be knighted by Hugh. Ultimately that request is denied, as Hugh cannot bring himself to strike the Sultan as part of the accolade ceremony. The captivity ends when Hugh makes a request to Saladin to be released, and amazingly the Sultan orders his own nobles to give the knight more than what was needed for payment of his ransom, so that Hugh is able to buy his freedom and even have money left over afterwards.

Though the poem is for the most part fictional, it is nevertheless a wonderful illustration of what it is to live as a Christian in a hostile culture. To impress the Muslim Sultan so much by Hugh's living example of chivalry, that Saladin himself would desire to become a knight - what a lesson to modern Christians of how to live a life so set apart from the world around us, that others would want to know what makes us different. And to offer such a Christian response in the face of captivity, that by the end it is the captors that pay for Hugh's release themselves - what a reminder that our response to hardship and difficulty can at times be much more powerful than spoken testimony.

Knights were expected to crave goodness and shun the temptations of the world; they were to prize honor and humility, and reject greed and evil. Knights were not perfect, but even when they fell short of the mark set for them, they did not lose their knighthood, but continued to strive towards their ultimate goal. Aren't we as Christians called in a similar fashion, to strive for ideals set forth by the laws of God, and to serve following the example of Christ Himself? Indeed, Jesus was the ultimate servant, as described in the Bible, "he made himself nothing by taking the very nature of a servant, being made in human likeness. And being found in appearance as a man, he humbled himself by becoming obedient to death — even death on a cross!" (Philippians 2:7-8, NIV).

Let us serve as prayer warriors, having no fear as we fight for the Kingdom of Heaven. The Bible is full of promises that the people of God do not battle alone, but that we are instead surrounded by the power of the Lord Most High, and nothing can stand against His mighty hand. The church is the Body of Christ, and Jesus proclaimed that even "the gates of hell shall not prevail against it" (Matthew 16:18, ESV).

Let us pray for faith, that we would trust in God's power above all else, remembering the story of the Prophet Elisha and his servant at a time of great need: "When the servant of the man of God got up and went out early the next morning, an army with horses and chariots had surrounded the city. 'Oh no, my lord! What shall we do?' the servant asked. 'Don't be afraid,' the prophet answered. 'Those who are with us are more than those who are with them.' And Elisha prayed, 'Open his eyes, Lord, so that he may see.' Then the Lord opened the servant's eyes, and he looked and saw the hills full of horses and chariots of fire all around Elisha" (2 Kings 6:15-17, ESV).

That same mighty power is available to us today. We have nothing to fear, for there is nothing that can stand against our God. We will find that the weapons of the enemy are much weaker than what we first imagined. Every battle belongs to the Lord, so let us kneel in worship, ready to serve our Master and fight for the Kingdom of Heaven.

Let us kneel as humble servants - not worthy by our own power or will, but transformed and made worthy by the sacrifice of Christ, our Prince of Peace. In His kingdom, Jesus says, "the greatest among you should be like the youngest, and the one who rules like the one who serves. For who is greater, the one who is at the table or the one who serves? Is it not the one who is at the table? But I am among you as one who serves. You are those who have stood by me in my trials. And I confer on you a kingdom, just as my Father conferred one on me, so that you may eat and drink at my table in my kingdom" (Luke 22:26-30, NIV).

Now being found worthy in Christ, we gladly kneel to worship and serve the Lord. Now having a purpose and a place at the King's table, let us offer our lives in worship and service for something greater than ourselves - let us live for His Kingdom and His glory. Let us kneel before our God in worship.

Proposal

So Jacob served seven years for Rachel,
and they seemed to him but a few days
because of the love he had for her.
(Genesis 29:20, ESV)

Is there anything as sweet as young love? New relationships hold the promise of a future together, for a family, and for growing old together. In our modern culture, there comes a time in every courtship when couples begin planning for their next steps, as their lives grow more and more entwined. During that time, there is an upwelling of emotion, hopes, and dreams - like a slow-building crescendo moving towards the covenant of marriage. And one of the most important steps along this journey is the engagement proposal.

Perhaps it comes as part of an elaborately prepared surprise, perhaps it is a spontaneous action, or perhaps it is something in-between. But at the simplest level, the classic proposal involves an engagement ring and a question: "Will you marry me?" The prospective groom, who promises to be provider and protector, will get down on one knee, in a posture of humble love before the woman he wants to marry. He asks her to spend her life with him, and gives her an engagement ring as a token of his commitment. He promises to love and cherish her, and to be faithful to her, through the good times and the bad, through sickness and health, for all the years that they will share together.

When a man kneels to propose, what kind of message is he communicating through his posture? He is physically demonstrating humility, and his body language is saying, "I will give you all of me." He proclaims that he will devote himself to his one true love, and that he will make her first in all relationships, shunning all others. He is making a lifelong commitment to serve her, protect her, and be with her, until death do they part.

A quick search of the Internet will produce countless proposal stories - some notable for their extravagance, others for their massive failure. It is clear that men all over the world will spend a lot of time and energy preparing huge displays of affection for this one moment. However, what is not so clear is how much of an effect such an expensive or over-the-top display will have on whether the woman involved actually accepts the proposal. Whether expressed simply in a quiet corner, or written in the sky with giant letters by a plane, the basic content of the question, 'will you marry me', does not change. That being said, it must feel wonderful to be the recipient of such a big display of affection - to know that someone thought so highly of you, that they created such an elaborate presentation to show the full extent of their love.

Therefore, how marvelous and wonderful it is that God has made the ultimate display of affection towards us, through the Crucifixion. What could be more costly or expensive than the death of Jesus Christ, the only begotten Son of God? The lynchpin of the entire redemption story, prophesied about since the fall of Man, no other act could possibly compare to the sacrifice of His Beloved Son. It is the most supreme and absolute exhibition of love that has ever been committed: "For God so loved the world that he gave his one and only Son, that whoever believes in him shall not perish but have eternal life" (John 3:16, NIV).

Whenever we fall short and feel unworthy of our salvation, we can look to the Cross and forever know that the love that sent our Savior to die for us is stronger than any sin for which we could be condemned. The Bible gives us this reassurance: "Therefore, there is now no condemnation for those who are in Christ Jesus, because through Christ Jesus the law of the Spirit who gives life has set you free from the law of sin and death" (Romans 8:1-2, NIV). We know that God will not reject us, having sacrificed so much for us out of His great love. We no longer need to fear judgment, damnation, or abandonment, for we are truly and deeply loved, and as the Word tells us, "There is no fear in love" (1 John 4:18, NIV).

Through the sacrifice made on the Cross, God has declared that we have now been made perfect in His sight, and that He will protect and honor us as His beloved. And in the face of such brazen love, what should our response be? The only response we could possibly have is to worship, to kneel before the Lord as a display of our commitment to Him in return.

When we kneel before our God, is the purpose any different than that of a man proposing to the woman he loves? Isn't the intent the same - to serve, to be faithful, and to love forever? And so in worship, we humbly kneel before the One we love, the One we are devoting our lives to, the One whose power will redefine and transform our lives. We commit ourselves to the Lord, to whom we belong, forsaking all others, for the rest of our lives, and for all eternity. Let us kneel in worship before the God who first loved us, and who we love in return.

Fall Face Down

When all the people of Israel
saw the fire come down
and the glory of the Lord on the temple,
they bowed down with their faces
to the ground on the pavement
and worshiped and gave thanks to the Lord,
saying, "For he is good,
for his steadfast love endures forever."
(2 Chronicles 7:3, ESV)

To prostrate is to lay down flat on the ground in deep reverence - perhaps it is an action that has become unfamiliar in our modern culture, but it is a form of worship with deep Biblical roots. Historically, many cultures around the globe would have been familiar with the act, as examples can be found in writings, paintings, and artifacts from all over the world. Even today, there are many religious sects that have retained the tradition of falling prostrate, one example being that of Catholic officers performing the posture during special ceremonies.

Prostration involves falling completely onto the ground, and putting your face on the floor as a sign of utter humility before the person being worshipped. With your entire body laying as flat as possible, there is no lower you could stoop, and it symbolizes that the person being bowed to is so much higher than ourselves. It is the response that the people of Israel would have in the presence of the Shekhinah Glory of God: "Fire came out from the presence of the Lord and consumed the burnt offering and the fat portions on the alter. And when all the people saw it, they shouted for joy and fell facedown" (Leviticus 9:24, NIV). Though perhaps no longer commonplace, the act of prostration is powerful, and full of meaning and significance.

Perhaps the most relatable illustration of this ritual in our modern culture is the act of kissing the ground when returning to home soil - an example of this comes from the Iranian Hostage Crisis. In the late 1970's, the nation of Iran was in the midst of a political revolution, which ultimately led to the ouster of the last Persian monarch, Shah Mohammad Reza Pahlavi, and the institution of an Islam-based theocratic government. This change in leadership brought that country into conflict with the United States, which had been supportive of the Shah's rule.

This conflict slowly grew in intensity, until finally bursting on November 4, 1979. On that day, the US Embassy, located in the city of Tehran, was taken over by Iranian revolutionaries and paramilitary personnel. The Americans who were in the embassy, fifty-two men and women, were then forcibly held in Iran for a period of 444 days. During that time, there were negotiations and rescue attempts to try to end the hostage situation, including a failed military operation that led to the tragic deaths of eight American servicemen in an aircraft accident. For well over a year, these hostages were completely at the mercy of their captors, never knowing what the day held for them – they were continuously moved around to different locations, put in solitary confinement, beaten and bound, and constantly threatened with death and torture.

Fortunately, through a long and laborious negotiation process, a deal was finally made between the two countries, and on January 20, 1981, the hostages were at last released from Iran. They were first flown to Algeria (which had assisted in the negotiations between the US and Iran), then to West Germany, and then finally arrived at a military base in the State of New York. Once they reached American soil at long last, several of the hostages, overjoyed to be free and now able to put this nightmare behind them, got on their knees and kissed the ground.

What an illustration of joy at the moment their freedom was complete, knowing that they would never be taken back to Iranian imprisonment. These newly freed men and women must have felt so many emotions going through their hearts - appreciation for their country that did not forget them, thankfulness to a government that had worked tirelessly to bring them home, and indebtedness to the military personnel who had perished attempting to rescue them - heroes who had given the ultimate sacrifice, but who the hostages would never be able to personally acknowledge.

What a picture of gratitude and freedom that in so many ways mirror our own hearts as we worship the Lord. Those who were once captives to sin are now set free. Those who were once filled with fear and uncertainty are now filled with hope and peace. Freedom for the hostages came at a heavy cost, and our freedom came through the sacrifice that Christ made on the Cross. Our response should be the same as theirs, to fall face down as we gratefully worship at the feet of the Lord.

We see a similar posture in the Book of Luke, from someone who was so overwhelmed by grace that she falls before Jesus. But rather than kissing the ground, this woman instead kisses the feet of the Messiah. "When one of the Pharisees invited Jesus to have dinner with him, he went to the Pharisee's house and reclined at the table. A woman in that town who lived a sinful life learned that Jesus was eating at the Pharisee's house, so she came there with an alabaster jar of perfume. As she stood behind him at his feet weeping, she began to wet his feet with her tears. Then she wiped them with her hair, kissed them and poured perfume on them" (Luke 7:36-38, NIV).

This woman knew that she did not deserve grace or mercy from God, so she did not try to justify herself before Jesus. Instead, she performed this humbling act as her penance, to show her repentance while being watched by those who were silently judging her. The other guests obviously knew who she was, and we can clearly feel from the text that she was not welcome in the house of Simon, who was a Pharisee, a group that emphasized adherence to religious law. She was uninvited, yet she felt compelled to come, even though it meant that she would be breaking cultural rules and social norms of the day. Unafraid of shame and scandal, there was nothing that was going to stop her from getting close to the Savior.

Jesus knew that the dinner party's host was appalled by her presence and by her act, and so turned to him and offered a parable for Simon's consideration. "'Two people owed money to a certain moneylender. One owed him five hundred denarii, and the other fifty. Neither of them had the money to pay him back, so he forgave the debts of both. Now which of them will love him more?' Simon replied, 'I suppose the one who had the bigger debt forgiven.' 'You have judged correctly,' Jesus said" (Luke 7:41-43, NIV). The Messiah identifies both debtors as having received grace and mercy, and juxtaposes the one who had the larger debt with the sinful woman. Simon's correct response to the question posed to him shows that he understood how grace works, but yet he fails to apply the principles of grace to the situation unfolding right in his own home.

In a room scandalized by her mere presence, she enters in nameless, but with her reputation proceeding her. She is set apart in the narrative from the other dinner guests by being described as having lived a sinful life, but the truth is that they all shared in that same accusation, as do we. What actually set her apart from the others was the fact that she was the only one that truly recognized her sinful nature, and understood her need for salvation. Everyone else at Simon's house looked at her and saw a sinner; Jesus looked at her and saw a daughter of God, someone worthy of redemption.

Jesus does not condemn the woman, but offers forgiveness in return for her faith put into action. "Then he turned toward the woman and said to Simon, 'Do you see this woman? I came into your house. You did not give me any water for my feet, but she wet my feet with her tears and wiped them with her hair. You did not give me a kiss, but this woman, from the time I entered, has not stopped kissing my feet. You did not put oil on my head, but she has poured perfume on my feet. Therefore, I tell you, her many sins have been forgiven—as her great love has shown'" (Luke 7:44-47, NIV). What an illustration of amazing grace – those who are self-righteous cannot comprehend it, but it draws in the lost and broken. The God who makes this kind of grace possible is so worthy of falling down before in worship.

The Lord deserves our absolute everything in worship - body, mind, heart and soul. He will not share that which is due to Him alone with any other. The Bible warns us, "Do not worship any other god, for the Lord, whose name is Jealous, is a jealous God" (Exodus 34:14, NIV). He singularly deserves high praise, as it is written, "I am the Lord; that is my name! I will not yield my glory to another or my praise to idols" (Isaiah 42:8, NIV).

Even other gods in the time of ancient Israel would fall humbly before the Lord, as this story from the Old Testament tells us: "When the Philistines captured the ark of God, they brought it from Ebenezer to Ashdod. Then the Philistines took the ark of God and brought it into the house of Dagon and set it up beside Dagon. And when the people of Ashdod rose early the next day, behold, Dagon had fallen face downward on the ground before the ark of the Lord. So they took Dagon and put him back in his place. But when they rose early on the next morning, behold, Dagon had fallen face downward on the ground before the ark of the Lord, and the head of Dagon and both his hands were lying cut off on the threshold. Only the trunk of Dagon was left to him" (1 Samuel 5:1-4, ESV).

The statue of this pretender god was made by human hands from rock, metal, or wood, and was utterly powerless - but still our Living God would not tolerate the idea of this created thing receiving worship from anyone, even the pagan Philistines, and therefore it had to be destroyed. And the Lord continues to blast idols today, wrecking anything that would take the attention of His people away from Himself. This is the awesome, jealous glory of God, unyielding in majesty - the Lord does not suffer any other gods, as He commands, "You shall have no other gods before me" (Exodus 20:3, NIV). He will humble all who come before Him, and all must acknowledge His greatness. We are called to worship Him alone, "For great is the Lord and most worthy of praise; he is to be feared above all gods" (Psalms 96:4, NIV).

Let us fall prostrate before the Lord, the Mighty One, in awe of His greatness, and in awe of His mercy and grace. We are not worthy to come close to the Holy God, but somehow through the Cross we find ourselves able to pass into His presence. No posture would be more natural and appropriate then to fall face down in pure worship. Let us fall down and kiss the feet of Jesus Christ.

We are nothing compared to the Lord of Lords and the King of Kings. Our hearts declare it, our songs of praise declare it, and when we prostrate before God, our bodies declare it. Let us fall at His feet and worship. Let us bow down.

> *Oh come, let us worship and bow down;*
> *let us kneel before the Lord, our Maker!*
> *(Psalms 95:6, ESV)*

HOW GOD MOVES

For I am the Lord your God
who takes hold of your right hand
and says to you,
Do not fear; I will help you.
(Isaiah 41:13, NIV)

Worship is always a response - a response to who God is and what He has done. He first loved us, and we respond to that love by accepting Him as our Savior and Lord. As the Bible says, "We love because he first loved us" (1 John 4:19, ESV). God is the One who made the first move. In worship, we might not even be the ones to initiate the singing, as the Lord is described as actually singing to us. "The Lord your God is in your midst, a mighty one who will save; he will rejoice over you with gladness; he will quiet you by his love; he will exult over you with loud singing" (Zephaniah 3:17, ESV). We respond by singing back to Him with songs of praise, lifting up the Name that is above all other names.

The preceding chapters examined a few pictures of what the posture of praise looks like from the worshipper's perspective, but now let us turn the point of view around. The Bible is filled with descriptions of the way that the Lord moves towards us, and examples of God's body language to His people. He searches for us, wrestles with us, and covers us as our Father. "How precious is your steadfast love, O God! The children of mankind take refuge in the shadow of your wings" (Psalms 36:7, ESV). Let us examine how God moves towards His people to expand our understanding of God's heart and loving kindness, and let us respond to Him with greater and deeper worship.

Washing Our Feet

Hundreds of years before the birth of Christ, the prophet Isaiah described Jesus as a servant; specifically as a suffering servant. "After he has suffered, he will see the light of life and be satisfied; by his knowledge my righteous servant will justify many, and he will bear their iniquities" (Isaiah 53:11, NIV). Though Jesus should have been honored throughout His time on Earth as the Son of God, He did not seek after worldly glory. Instead, Christ humbled Himself to show us that we should give of ourselves, and live everyday in service to God and to others. "For even the Son of Man did not come to be served, but to serve, and to give his life as a ransom for many" (Mark 10:45, NIV).

Before going to the Cross, Jesus enjoyed one last evening with His disciples, and used the opportunity to teach them what it really means to be a servant. To these twelve men, He was their rabbi, or teacher, and they had learned so much from Jesus over the course of several years - through His words, actions, and miracles. He had redefined every aspect of their lives, and changed their very understanding of reality. But for this last object lesson, the Messiah took on a task that was incredibly below the status of a rabbi, and it was shocking for the disciples to see. "He laid aside his outer garments, and taking a towel, tied it around his waist. Then he poured water into a basin and began to wash the disciples' feet and to wipe them with the towel that was wrapped around him" (John 13:4-5, ESV).

This act left the disciples confused, and they were not sure how to react. The washing of feet was a task usually delegated to a servant or other low-level household member. But to these twelve men who had followed Him daily for the preceding few years, Jesus was more than just a man - He was the one who had opened their eyes and their hearts to the truths of the Kingdom of Heaven, truths that they knew no mere rabbi could have taught them. It would have been one thing for a human teacher to serve them in this way, but the disciples knew Jesus to be so much more than that, as the Apostle Peter had previously professed, "You are the Christ, the Son of the living God" (Matthew 16:16, ESV).

Knowing their confusion, Jesus explained

the lesson to them after completing the cleaning ritual. "When he had washed their feet and put on his outer garments and resumed his place, he said to them, 'Do you understand what I have done to you? You call me Teacher and Lord, and you are right, for so I am. If I then, your Lord and Teacher, have washed your feet, you also ought to wash one another's feet. For I have given you an example, that you also should do just as I have done to you'" (John 13:12-15, ESV).

If Jesus - the Messiah, the Prince of Peace, the Son of God, and the head of the Church - chose to live as a lowly servant, then those who proclaim Christ as Lord have no other choice but to follow His lead and practice this same kind of humble servitude as well. The command to put others before ourselves is found throughout the New Testament, as we are called to "Submit to one another out of reverence for Christ" (Ephesians 5:21, NIV). Let us honor the example that Jesus lays out before us and live in humility. Let us remember that our lives are not about us - indeed, our lives are now set apart solely for glorifying the Lord - soli Deo gloria.

Jesus laid down His life for others as the ultimate act of love, and all Christians are called to respond in the same way. "My command is this: Love each other as I have loved you. Greater love has no one than this: to lay down one's life for one's friends" (John 15:12-13, NIV). God loved us, so that we can know love - Jesus served us, so we must also serve others.

By living in this way, not only do we offer our help to others, but in addition to that, our humble service identifies us as the people of God to the unbelieving world. As Jesus said, "By this all people will know that you are my disciples, if you have love for one another" (John 13:35, ESV). Our witness to those who have not yet received His salvation does not require words; we can share our living testimony of the redeeming love of God just by living as humble servants. Therefore, let us serve others as an act of worship to the Lord.

He Runs to Us

God is described throughout the Scriptures as our Heavenly Father, and in the culture in which the Bible was written, fathers were respected without question by their children. This is reflected in the Ten Commandments - God's law given to Moses and the nation of Israel, which provided the very foundation for Jewish society, the impact of which is still felt in our culture today. The sixth commandment declares, "Honor your father and your mother" (Exodus 20:12a, NIV). It is the first of the commandments to deal with interpersonal relationships, and it came with a promise attached: "so that you may live long in the land the Lord your God is giving you" (Exodus 20:12b, NIV).

The parable of the Prodigal Son centers around a young man who defied these cultural norms, shunned his father's love, and selfishly demanded that which did not belong to him. "There was a man who had two sons. The younger one said to his father, 'Father, give me my share of the estate'" (Luke 15:11-12, NIV). This was more than an innocent request for money. In fact, it is widely interpreted as the son wishing that his father was already dead - a grave insult to any parent. Shockingly, the father capitulates to the demand and gives the son what he wants, a plot twist that was unimaginable to the original audience. Not long after, the son squanders the ill-gotten wealth by chasing after temporary pleasures, what Jesus described as 'wild living', and he predictably falls into a hopeless situation.

He realizes that the only way for him to survive is to go back to his father on his knees, and so he turns to go back home. The son was not sure what to expect upon arrival, and so he began to prepare a hasty apology. He did not hope to regain his status as a son or heir, not after what he had done - the most he was hoping for was to be hired as one of the workers on the father's estate. It is at this point in the narrative that the true heart of the father is revealed, as the story continues: "But while he was still a long way off, his father saw him and was filled with compassion for him; he ran to his son, threw his arms around him and kissed him" (Luke 15:20, NIV).

In an honor-based culture and society, respected landowners such as the father in this story were expected to act with distinction at all times while out in public. But this father threw all of that aside when he saw his son returning home, and ran to him, not caring what anyone watching might have thought. The love that the father had for his lost son was so great that all pride and status became nothing compared to the desire to embrace his child.

Jesus shared this parable, the last in a series about finding things that were lost, to teach us how great the love of God is. The story paints a clear picture that every time a sinner repents and returns home, the joy and delight in receiving them back is great enough to make God run. This is the Lord of Lords, the King of Kings, the Creator of Heaven and Earth - yet all that status is laid aside by the Father's heart. The father in the story immediately begins preparing a celebratory feast upon his son's return, which is only a glimpse of the joy there is in Heaven for every person who turns away from sin. As Jesus tells us, "there is rejoicing in the presence of the angels of God over one sinner who repents" (Luke 15:10, NIV).

Our Heavenly Father is scanning the horizon, looking for His lost children returning home. Just like the Prodigal Son, those who were lost fear that they may face rejection upon arrival, but instead God offers acceptance to all who repent. The Lord receives us with open arms, and just like the father in the story, He says, "'Let's have a feast and celebrate. For this son of mine was dead and is alive again; he was lost and is found'" (Luke 15:24, NIV). The Father is looking for us, the Father sees us coming from a long way off, the Father runs to us, the

Father throws His arms around us and kisses us, and celebrates with all of Heaven. Let us worship our Good Father.

Arms Wide Open

As we meditate on how we surrender before the Lord, we remember that it was Christ who first surrendered to His Father's will, costly and painful as it was. Before the crucifixion, He asked for another way, pleading, "'Father, if you are willing, take this cup from me'" (Luke 22:42, NIV). But ultimately, in faithful obedience and in fulfilment of prophecy, Jesus opened His arms on the Cross and gave up His life so that we may live. Out of His great love for us, and though we did not deserve it, the Lord made a way for us to be saved. As the Bible says, "But God demonstrates his own love for us in this: While we were still sinners, Christ died for us" (Romans 5:8, NIV).

God's Law made it clear that blood was required for the atonement of sins, as was evident from some of the earliest portions of the Old Testament, in which many different kinds of animal sacrifices were outlined. "In fact, the law requires that nearly everything be cleansed with blood, and without the shedding of blood there is no forgiveness" (Hebrews 9:22, NIV). However, the Jewish sacrificial system was just a placeholder and not meant to be a permanent solution, as it is written, "It is impossible for the blood of bulls and goats to take away sins" (Hebrews 10:4, NIV). The burden placed upon Jesus was great - to absolve the transgressions of all mankind, as a free gift of grace to anyone who would seek salvation by believing in Him as Savior. No other offering or sacrifice would be sufficient for the task.

Only the blood of Christ was strong enough to cleanse the stain of our iniquities, because of how tarnished our souls had become: "Though your sins are like scarlet, they shall be as white as snow" (Isaiah 1:18, NIV). Like a lamb being led to slaughter, Jesus went willingly to Calvary, and on the Cross, "he bowed his head and gave up his spirit" (John 19:30, NIV). In a posture of absolute love, with arms nailed wide open and head bowed with thorny crown, the Son of God died for our sake.

Jesus paid it all, He was the ransom for our redemption, and we can obtain eternal life through Christ alone. The Bible describes the great transaction for us: "But he was pierced for our transgressions, he was crushed for our iniquities; the punishment that brought us peace was on him, and by his wounds we are healed" (Isaiah 53:5, NIV). All that is required of us in order to receive this salvation is to simply believe, "For it is by grace you have been saved, through faith—and this is not from yourselves, it is the gift of God" (Ephesians 2:8, NIV).

Jesus made the way - He took the punishment that rightfully belonged to us, and forever freed us from sin and death. And now there is no one and nothing that can challenge our claim to salvation. "Who will bring any charge against those whom God has chosen? It is God who justifies. Who then is the one who condemns? No one. Christ Jesus who died—more than that, who was raised to life—is at the right hand of God and is also interceding for us" (Romans 8:33-34, NIV).

In light of this sacrifice, and of God's mercy and grace, the only response we could possibly have is to give our all back to Him. He deserves our whole lives, our whole passion, and our whole purpose. We look forward to the day when we will worship the Lord with all of creation, joining in the praise of the universe: "Then I heard every creature in heaven and on earth and under the earth and on the sea, and all that is in them, saying: 'To him who sits on the throne and to the Lamb be praise and honor and glory and power, FOR EVER AND EVER!" (Revelation 5:13, NIV).

A Call to Worship

Worship can take countless forms - as the glory of God is ever growing, so are the ways by which we can worship Him growing always. These short chapters ruminated on several interpretations of a few postures of praise, to hopefully expand our perspective of what more worship could be. But there are so many other illustrations of worship out there that call us to ever increase our adoration of the Lord. May we never stop finding new avenues by which we can praise Him deeper and more fully.

Worship is powerful - let us not forget the walls of Jericho, which were renowned during their time for their strength and impregnability. Remember that it was not weapons or armies that tore those mighty fortifications down. The people of God came to take the city with shouting and the sound of trumpets - worship brought down those walls. Let our worship tear down walls today - walls of sin, fear, doubt, and hate.

Worship will lead us closer to God. Often the body follows the heart, but sometimes the heart will follow the body. We all go through dry seasons of life where worship does not seem to flow freely, for whatever reason. Maybe the worries in our lives keep us from fully entering the thone room of God. It could be that the sins we hold on to are holding us back from the Lord. Perhaps you just feel distant from Him for no discernable reason. In those times, it may be that taking an intentional stance and actively posturing our bodies in praise can make all the difference in how our hearts respond to the call to worship.

The next time you enter into a time of sacred worship, try closing your eyes and see if you don't feel more focused. Stand on your feet to praise Him, and see if you don't feel more eager to see God move. Raise your hands in submission, and see if you don't feel more surrendered. Bow before the Lord, and see if you don't feel more humble. Offer your body as a living sacrifice to the Lord, holy and pleasing to God, and let true and proper worship flow from every part of your being.

Let us use all that we are to worship God, for He alone is truly worthy of all our praise.

Praise the Lord, my soul;
All my inmost being, praise his holy name.
(Psalms 103:1, NIV)

to J, C, and c - love always

REFERENCES

[i] Kansas Historical Society. www.kshs.org/kansa-pedia/philip-sheridan/17323

[ii] Leckie, Robert (1998). The Wars of America. Castle Books. p. 537. ISBN 0-7858-0914-7.

[iii] The Order of Chivalry. L'ordene de Chevalerie. Hammersmith : Kelmscott Press ; London : Sold by Reeves & Turner, 1893.

Contact Information
bodyworshipbook@gmail.com

Social Media
shine in the darkness

Made in the USA
Monee, IL
23 November 2021

82552814R00080